'Occasionally a narrative comes a
written, but extremely practica
message into one's own life. Such
Road to the Father's House.

'Based on the story of the prodigal son from the Bible in
Luke 15, this volume, skilfully incorporates allegory and
imagination, to help you walk in the footsteps of the leading
characters. You will experience their emotions and challenges,
enabling you to better assimilate these transforming principles
into your own heart and life, and fathom the profound depths
of the love of God.

'I have so enjoyed reading this volume and will be
recommending it to young and old alike who are passionate to
really know Him. This is a foundational message that indeed all
of us need to really "get".'
John Arnott, Catch The Fire World; author

'I love how Alistair writes. It's how he talks. Deep yet simple;
profound yet understandable. I was caught up in his narrative
and the journey he shares with us. *The Road to the Father's House*
is one that all of us who know Jesus are on, even if we didn't
know it. Jesus didn't tell us He was taking us to heaven; rather
to meet Father God. Well done, Alistair, on this project. You
are a brilliant author.'
Steve Long, Senior Leader, Catch The Fire Church (Toronto); author

'Grasping how much we are loved by the Father in heaven is a
revolutionary revelation with ever-increasing depths. Alistair
Forman unpacks not only intellectually but also on a heart level
how to journey from living as an orphan to identifying as a son
or daughter. Utilising gripping stories from his own experience
and the lives of others, Alistair brings home authentic truth
which has the capacity to change lives.

'For all who are ready to abandon the "pigs' trough" of
prodigal, orphan and living less than the Father's best, this book
will help transform you. For all who want "tools in your tool

belt" to help impart the revelation of the Father's love to others, this book is for you. For those who enjoy a good read and want to learn, this book is for you. For those who don't grasp what it means to have a heavenly Father, this book is for you.

'Let's just sum it up: this book is for everyone.'
Patricia Bootsma, author

'We first met Alistair when he was around fourteen and targeted him for a discipleship guinea pig. Oh dear. Thankfully, he has recovered from that process and then he dove head first into Jesus, encountered the fullness of the Trinity and has now become one of the most effective leaders in our world. When people hear him speak or receive his pastoring, they know they are loved and prioritised and that the next steps are clear.

'The striking reality of this book is the same as when you meet or are influenced by Alistair: you are stopped in your tracks by the anointing of authenticity, integrity and simplicity. He's lived a journey, he's on a journey, he leads people on journeys, and this book will do the same.

'This book is a journey into the Father's heart. But more than that, it's an invitation for you to go on a journey baptised, surrounded and encased by God's love and His revelation of who you are.

'God is interventional. This book is lovingly but authentically interventional. It will help you see where God has touched your past, invaded your present and, maybe more importantly, how the Father wants to take you by the hand and lead your future.

'From people who know there's more but haven't tasted that yet, to those who know who they are and have excluded themselves, this book has the potential to release a generation of empowered and grounded sons and daughters.

'Prepare for a God-empowered momentum in your heart and in your life!'
Stu and Chlo Glassborow, Lead Pastors, Catch The Fire London; founders, The Kenyan Children's Project

'Packed full of story and Scripture, *The Road to the Father's House* will take you on a personal journey of healing and discovery. An absolute gift to anyone who desires to drawer closer to the heart of God.'
Marie Aitken, Head of England, Alpha; founder, Girl Can Daily

'Alistair dares us to be the character of our story with God. No one talks about what the prodigal son had to do the next morning after the big party, but this book does. Being home, truly home, takes some getting used to. The kingdom of God is a party, but who is going to clean up afterwards? How do we now live as a son or daughter with Father? Alistair helps us see that we will want to help clean up because the party was for us and there will be party after party in the Father's house.

'Alistair does not give us any formulas for success. We like formulas because we think we can control them. We wish God had left us ten steps to happiness and seven steps to holiness, but He did not because He is after a relationship, which we can't control. We really can't control any relationship, any more than I can point the remote control at my wife and click her off. Don't try that at home. And our relationship with Father God is even more complicated, messy and wonderful.

'I think this book will make you homesick for the Father's house, which is the home you always wanted and always knew had to be there.'
W Andrew McMillan, Pastor Comunidad Cristiana de Fe, Medellín Colombia; author

'Often, when reading books by gifted authors, I have wondered as to their journey and process. How did the idea for the book come about? How did they begin the work? How did they persevere through the various iterations and drafts to arrive at the final product?

'In this particular instance, I have had the great pleasure of being able to see this project evolve from its inception, through to the finished copy you now hold in your hands. It has been a labour of love for Alistair, of this I am certain. His desire was to recount, through his own journey and experiences, the grace and goodness of God in his life – and this is what this book is: an honest, at times raw, but consistently authentic journey.

'I have often encouraged Alistair that his teaching and preaching carries with it something of the ability Jesus had to present wonderfully complex truths in accessible and beautiful ways. It has now become apparent to me that the ability Alistair has to do this in his teaching has translated across into his writing, and for this I am grateful. I found this book to be engaging and disarming in equal measure – whether it is an analogy from a Marvel film, or a unique perspective on one of the parables of Jesus, Alistair has a gift to be able to take a deep concept, and in a moment, make it accessible.

'I am confident this book will encourage you in a deep and profound way, and will inspire you to push deeper into the heart of God. I know nothing would make Alistair happier than to know, through telling his own story, that someone has been encouraged in their relationship with God – and I am confident this book will do exactly that.

Tom Allsop, Pastor, Catch The Fire Three Rivers

'*The Road to the Father's House* is a story wrapped in gentle theology. It is the story of a heart encountering the loving grace of our Father. This story includes each of us. Alistair Forman has a unique way of helping us through our pain and shame to embrace the heart of God. Reading this book, you will want to throw out all religious processes you have ever known, heard and attempted to incorporate into your life, and run unashamed into the embrace of Abba. Personally, I am now running faster than ever!'

Jay Snyder, Passion For Life Ministries

THE ROAD TO THE FATHER'S HOUSE

Where God's presence
meets your story

ALISTAIR FORMAN

instant
apostle

First published in Great Britain in 2021

Instant Apostle
104 The Drive
Rickmansworth
Herts
WD3 4DU

British Library Cataloguing-in-Publication Data

A catalogue record for this book is available from the British Library.

This book and all other Instant Apostle books are available from Instant Apostle:

Website: www.instantapostle.com
Email: info@instantapostle.com

ISBN 978-1-912726-47-9

Printed in Great Britain.

Dedication

To everyone who is walking their own journey back to the Father's house, perhaps limping or feeling the weight of their own limitations or mistakes, I dedicate this book to you. Your heavenly Father came running just for you, to bring you home as a whole, healed and redeemed child of His. There is a party in His house waiting for you.

I also dedicate this book to my son. Your mum and I are so proud of you. Your life is just beginning but your Father in heaven is already walking alongside you, talking to you, dreaming with you... and He has such sights to show you. Trust Him, He won't ever disappoint you.

Contents

Acknowledgements

This book is all about the decades' long journey we do with God over the course of our lives. The people who have stood by me on this journey are the ones who have kept me walking and kept me trusting when I would have bailed out or fallen by the wayside. God works through the people you have a five-minute chat with at the back of church on a Sunday morning. He moves through the person who gives you a cup of tea on your first night at a home group. The presence of heaven is there when you walk around the block with that mentor or leader and chat about your life. He moves through the person in front of you, the one doing the preaching and the one smiling at you in the car park, even though you can't remember their name. God has appointed hundreds of His children to help you and me along as we walk the journey of our life. Each one of them has played a part in helping you and me get this far.

I want to give thanks for all those pastors, vicars, youth leaders, elders and friends who have influenced my journey, kept me walking and kept me looking for God in the midst of my life. I honour you and thank you.

Stu and Chlo Glassborow, thank you for contending for me, growing me and loving me for all these years. You introduced me to the Father's love and to the supernatural God I'd only heard about before. You have changed my life forever. The hunger and desperation for God you live with has marked me so profoundly. You will see your fingerprints all over this book.

Tom Allsop, you were a father to me, then you made space for me to be your friend, and then you made it completely natural for me to be your colleague and co-worker in Christ. You have consistently encouraged me and called me higher, to be the person God made me to be. Everyone should have a friend like you.

Jay and Peg, thank you for introducing me to my wife, Abigail. Thank you for marrying us, mentoring us and modelling marriage, ministry and maturity in ways that have been so life-giving to us. You live with a hunger for God, an expectancy for Him to show up and do the miraculous, and yet you also have the heart to sit with people in their pain until they are loved back to life. I want to be like you when I grow up.

John and Carol Arnott, being one of your many, many spiritual grandkids spread across the globe is an utter privilege. The ministry you have stewarded since the outpouring in Toronto in 1994 has had the deepest impact on my life. Your humility in consistently pointing to Jesus and away from yourselves never ceases to amaze me. Thank you for the gospel values you have helped steward. I hope this book continues the spread of those truths of God's goodness and His nearness to us all.

To my Catch The Fire World family, thank you for all the sermons and the moments of revelation at all the conferences, Zoom calls and meetings. You are very dear to me. To my London church family, thank you for your constant love and encouragement over the years. I love you guys!

To all the incredible pastors and leaders who have endorsed me and this book, thank you. Emailing many of my heroes in the faith and asking for them to not only read my book but also say nice things about it was a test of my sonship in God – ironically what this whole book is about! I will treasure your gracious and kind words.

Mum and Dad, you have supported me all my life and you have always been there for me. Your generosity and patience towards me has made it possible to do and achieve things I never would have been able to by myself. I'm sure most of my school teachers would fall over if they found out I was releasing a book – thank you for always encouraging me to be the best I can be.

To my wife, Abigail, without whom this book would still likely be a couple of unfinished documents on a computer somewhere. You drew this out in me, you helped me tap into God's supply of courage and self-belief to get it done. You believed in me when I didn't think my story or my words were going to be of any interest or any help to anyone else. You also helped me remember to try to spell words properly and use grammar like a normal person. I love you for who you are most of all. Your devotion to God, to your family and to the one in front of you who needs love consistently undoes me. Thank you for saying yes to me.

Lastly and most importantly, to Father, Jesus and Holy Spirit. My God and my Lord. This book is about You, it is from You, it is for You and it is an offering to You. In this book I have tried to recount all the healing and all the goodness You have poured on me. I have not achieved that because the list is too long and the stories too numerous. I have seen the deaf hear and the blind see because of You, I've seen lives transformed and restored because You showed up. More than all those things, however, I have felt Your presence walking bedside me as we have walked the road back to Your house ever since the first day I met You. You have never left me, You have always loved me and I have nothing but gratitude and thanks to know that I am one of Your sons.

1
Welcome to Wherever You Are

You open your eyes.

Slowly.

You're a little disorientated at first; you feel good but you just can't quite remember where you are or maybe even who you are yet. Light is streaming through a gap in the curtains, a soft, hazy beam lancing its way across the room. A bedroom. The soft furnishings look inviting. A warm wing-backed, cushioned chair sits in one corner of the room, a simple wooden table and chair by the windowsill. Your favourite coat is hanging on the handle to the wardrobe. Did you put that there?

What did you do last night?

You don't really remember. You can't even recall getting into bed or changing.

It's only when you sit up that you realise just how comfortable this bed actually is. There's comfy and then there's this. It's got that feel of an old, well-used mattress, like the kind a grandma puts in the spare room for her grandchild to sleep and feel safe on. Propping yourself up, you gently lean back against the cushioned headboard and pull your knees up to your chest. Your eyes slowly pan around the room.

Your room.

It's warm. Feels safe.

It somehow feels familiar and yet unfamiliar at the same time. It's unusual, because you don't recall having a lot of history living in this room... but it has the signs of your life in it. Photos in frames, your slippers by the bed, your favourite mug on the table. It's even got a candle with the smell you like hidden somewhere in here.

You rub your eyes, half-expecting the scene to disappear and be replaced by something more familiar.

It doesn't disappear.

You're here.

This is your room.

It feels good to be here… really good, in fact.

You can't even rationalise in your head why it feels so good and right, it just does.

Inside you there are emotions bubbling up and neurones firing in your brain. Ideas, confidence, hope, excitement, anticipation, peace, expectancy… you name it. It's like just being here is uncapping something.

'What is this place?' you whisper out loud. 'How did I get here?'

The parable of the prodigal son is one of the most well-known stories Jesus told. The life-changing message the parable brings us is what this book is all about, but it's my question about it that we're really going to spend our time on.

What if there were a sequel to the story?

What if the narrative just… kept going?

What if Jesus had continued, extended the parable and added another chapter in His tale of the two sons and their father?

If you think I'm going to suggest that we start adding things into the Bible, rest easy, I'm not going there. I am wondering out loud, though. What would it have been like if Jesus had kept the narrative going and as Act 1, 'The redemption', drew to a close, Act 2, 'The living of it', began?

Let's back up a bit first. The parable of the prodigal son is found in Luke 15. You should open a Bible and read it if you never have. It is exceptional and yet so simple. A son takes his inheritance early, basically tells his dad he wishes he were dead, flees the father's home, loses everything he has and hits the lowest depths of shame imaginable. Then, one day, after coming to his senses, he takes the long path home that leads to the road to his father's house, and while 'still a long way off' (v20), is met by his father in a collision of grace that he never saw coming. Just when you think it is all done, a third character enters the story. An older brother. He can't handle his younger brother's return, or his redemption. He too experiences his father coming out to him to rescue him from himself. Both children receive this love, one accepts it and the other... well, we never find out what his response is.

So much of the Old Testament and the New is found in this one little story. The story has given hope and life to millions of people since the day Jesus told it. There's something about it, though; even when I consider that all Scripture is 'God-breathed' (2 Timothy 3:16, NIV), this parable seems to stand by itself as something particularly special.

We have a father meeting His sons on the paths of their brokenness. There are tears and hugs, then a cloak and a ring that appear out of nowhere to cover all the shame. We have the same father offering both children a way back home. A walk home, side by side with him. An opportunity to be restored. A chance to talk about every wound and cut and grief. An offer to cross the threshold of their father's house as fully empowered and renewed sons of the house. It is beautiful, it's simple and it's profound.

For so many Jesus followers throughout history, this parable has become personal. It's not a story about some historical figure, some foolish disciple who should have known better, or some Old Testament king who didn't get it. It's a story about me and about you.

This story gets under my skin more than any other Jesus told.

I'll be honest, this story has always left me feeling so utterly exposed and convicted by the weakness, the pride and the selfishness of those two sons.

They are me.

So completely me.

Their sin-covered rags and masks are mine. The paths they walked down are my paths. The trenches they fell in are my trenches. I've hidden down the same alleys and in the middle of the same crowds as them both. I've thought the same thoughts and yearned for the same things. I've justified the same actions. I've walked away from the Father and questioned His way of doing things, just like they did. I've needed to be rescued from the world and from myself, just as they did too.

However, even in the midst of all these thoughts, I have found that the story is more than just a means for us to associate and empathise with a human struggle. There's something far greater going on.

This story is a window into the heart of God as a father.

Unfortunately, for so many of us the window that we were meant to look through as we see Him has been stained and tarnished, and He has been misrepresented for far too long. This parable sets the story straight on who God the Father is. I think Jesus knew full well when He told this parable that He was drawing us, His listeners, to consider the rawest expressions of our human brokenness and our choices, while also side-swiping us with the reality of the unrelenting, unmerited, grace-driven love of God the Father towards us all. For the listeners, for us, we are left with the thought: If the father – representing God Himself – was willing to rescue and rebuild those two boys at their worst, maybe He would rescue us too, no matter what?

I think Jesus meant for us to see it this way. I believe He meant for us to see the real us, before the real God, and for that thought to stop us in our tracks. What we do from that point is up to us. We can shrug it off, we can take a few moments to think about it and then get on with our lives. Or we can get the tent out and camp in it, give it time and allow all that revelation a chance to change us.

As I've journeyed with this story and its implications over the years, I have struggled to move past it. There has always been something present in the back of my mind; a question: What happened next? Rescue and redemption are profoundly important moments… but something happens after that, right? The story keeps going, doesn't it?

So what happened next? Because I'm living the 'next' right now; it's my life. If you're a follower of Jesus, it's your life too. If you're not, I invite you right now to make your own choice about Jesus and the Father He wants to introduce you to. I experienced the loving redemption of the Father when I first really gave my life to Jesus. It was a moment of grace; that means unmerited favour was shown to me, I was given something for free that I didn't earn or deserve. Mercy was shown to me for everything I had done to hurt God, others and myself. I was forgiven. I was set free. I was cleansed and washed of all the toxic thoughts and choices I'd made over the years. I honestly can't quite describe the totality of the impact it made on my life; I can only say it changed everything in me forever. I was a redeemed person. My life purchased and made completely new.

Following hot on the heels of that moment, however, was this question, 'How do I live now that I am redeemed… how do I be that new person?'

What comes next…?

Jesus told a lot of parables, relatable stories, basically, to those who listened to Him. He spoke about feasts, the buying of precious pearls, what to do with the talents you've been given, or the vineyard you've been entrusted with. He told many powerful stories, but honestly, I've never dwelt on what may have come next in them. They felt contained and finished, Jesus' point clearly made and delivered. This one, however, this tale of a father and his sons, though complete and perfectly presented for its listeners, always felt to me as if it invited us to inhabit it and build on it. The story almost seems to hang in mid-air, because so much has happened, but there surely must be so much more to come.

I needed to hear what the father's next words were. What was that walk home back to the house like? What did the father and redeemed son talk about on that walk? Did they speak about why the son had left, where the roots to his insecurity lay, or did they just take in the scenery as they made their way home?

What would it be like for the redeemed child to walk back into his bedroom, cleaned and tidied ready for his return? What would it be like to live out the next few days and weeks from that moment as a new person? What more was this incredible father going to reveal to his children to help them believe what had always been true about them and, indeed, about himself?

All of these questions have swirled around my head for years. In the pages to come we're going to try to answer some of them. Now, the truth is that all of Scripture speaks to each one of these questions, the Bible is not silent on these issues or on my questions. The Gospels of Jesus' life show us Jesus, the source of all our freedom. Romans 8 speaks of our adoption as God's sons. Colossians 1 and 3 speak of our oneness with God, our new fused nature with Him. Galatians 3 reminds us that we'll never need to try to earn something we actually were given as a gift through grace. The entire book of Acts shows us the power and wonders that follow those who believe they are who God says they are. The book of Revelation shows where it's all heading.

So even though the Bible isn't silent on my questions, I could see that this parable of Jesus created an opportunity for us all to become a character and member of the cast, and ask our questions from that place. This parable reveals the father heart of God towards us on our worst day, and so the outworking of that revelation is for us to live, no longer as spiritual orphans, but as fathered sons and daughters. It has to be personal.

As I saw myself so clearly in this story, I wanted the questions to be answered from within it too. A soteriological explanation from a theologian's dissertation about the nature of the sanctified life was not going to speak to my heart. I needed to see Father God turn to His formerly prodigal son with His arm round his shoulder and speak to Him in that whisper of love.

What happens next, after God has met us in a grace collision of forgiveness and restoration, is of supreme importance to each one of us. What we do with it, where we go with it, who we choose to be as a result of that moment, are some of the most important questions we will ever engage with in life.

So as we go forward from this moment, we will be camping around the identity and belonging that gets released into our lives as a result of that grace collision with the Father. This book is about what it looks like to be adopted into God's family, with all our history and baggage, and yet be treated like a birth child with all the privileges and intimacy that comes with that.

The journey we're in and the one that lies ahead

Spiritually speaking, before we know God, before we have that encounter with Jesus Christ that changes everything, we are like orphans. We're just trying to figure out where we came from, what we're on this planet to do and pretty much making it up as we go along. We don't know who we are or whose we are.

Identity is probably one of the most talked about issues of our times, and for good reason. We all have a need in our very blood to know who we are, why we are the way that we are and what we are here on this planet for. Four of the biggest questions of any human worldview are: Where did I come from, what does it mean to be alive, how do I differentiate between right and wrong, and where am I going? They are all questions that need an answer.

Many try to figure out their identity questions by allying themselves to a movement or a cultural expression. Many identities are forged based on feelings: 'I feel, therefore I am.' Some people root themselves in the family name, or history and traditions. Some of this stuff can be good and can help us – we feel belonging and find our tribe. Some of it is just smoke and vapours and doesn't have the depth or grounding to actually be useful. Much of it is simply toxic and will take us to a far-off country where no one even knows the Father's name, let alone cares what He thinks. None of these things ultimately can answer the deepest questions of our hearts, nor provide the truth of who we really are.

One of the primary roles a father often plays in a healthy family unit is to provide identity to the children. Mothers lead in giving the child unconditional, nurturing love, whereas the father imbues a sense of who they are in this world. Growing up as a young boy, when I was hurt or sick at school I wanted my mum to come rescue me and look after me; I wanted that nurture love she would bring. When I started getting older and was trying to understand who I was in the world, it was my dad I looked to and went to. Parents get to play an incredible role in shaping their children.

Now I'm definitely thinking more of Mufasa speaking to Simba on Pride Rock in *The Lion King* about who he was and his future as a king, rather than Darth Vader in *Star Wars* revealing to a one-handed Luke Skywalker that he's actually his dad and he'd like to team up and take over the universe together (although, fun fact, both are voiced by the same actor). My point is, earthly fathers are meant to do this identity-affirming and imparting role because it is a reflection of what our heavenly Father does at a much deeper, more profound level. We all need to hear the words our heavenly Father speaks over us.

The most healed, free and whole people I've ever met on planet Earth are those who have experienced fathering from Father God. Regardless of how well they were or weren't brought up, it is the affirming voice of their heavenly Dad that brings the truest revelation of their identity as son or daughter.

The opposite of knowing and believing you're part of God's family is spiritual orphanness. This is what happens when that heavenly fathering is not experienced or known. It is where there is an absence of the good and true Father to tell you who you are, whose you are and what on earth you're here for. As in the natural, when we spiritually don't know we have a father who is good and loves us, we act like orphans, trying to seek that love or identity from anywhere that might offer it. Adam and Eve looked for it in a piece of fruit (Genesis 3:6). Their son Cain tried to find it in favour and being the best (Genesis 4:3). The hundreds of Bible pages after their stories tell of so many others who tried to find their identity and belonging in places other than God.

Spiritual orphanness is not something that you can avoid just because you're a Christian or a godly person. I know, because I thought that being a Christian and a member of the club would fix me overnight of all my dysfunctions. As it turns out, all my worst behaviour, all my abandonment and justifying, the pride, the selfishness, my fleeing and all the people pleasing I've ever done didn't disappear overnight. They all found their root in insecurities around who I was and whose I was. When I made a full commitment to follow God as a teenager, I accepted the gift He offered willingly, but there was still so much I didn't know about Him. I didn't believe it yet that this God was a good Dad who actually wanted to get down in the dirt with me. So I spent a long time trying to measure up to who I thought He wanted me to be. I was a Christian but still acting like an orphan.

God is a good father, and that therefore makes us sons and daughters, free and whole in Him (Romans 8:15-17). Jesus, God's perfect Son, lived His life only doing and saying what He saw the Father doing (John 5:19) and one day, when the time came for Him to answer the reason for all His ministry and purpose on earth, Jesus simply said that He was 'the way'. The way, not just to heaven. The way, not just to eternal life. Jesus was and is the way to the Father (John 14:6). The Father, being with Him, knowing Him and being known by Him... it is the goal as far as Jesus is concerned.

This revelation was a life-changer for me. Before I really gave my life to God, my life goal was just about making sure I shaped up when I needed to, slacked off when I could get away with it and avoided trouble, and I ended up disappointing everyone. Once I became a Christian I felt much better about who I was and excited to know and experience God, but I was still just trying to make the whole thing work without letting Him down… especially after all He'd done for me. I knew I owed Him, I knew I needed to shape up and work hard. I had been given a ticket to heaven and I needed to show I was worthy of it. Right?

When this life-changer revelation that Jesus *was the way to the Father* hit me square between the eyes, I suddenly realised how much more there was of God that I hadn't taken hold of. I'd seen Jesus as the One who gave me my 'get out of jail free' card for my sins and that golden ticket to heaven one day. I'd also seen Him as a blocker-type figure, holding the Father back from beating me up long enough for me to get into eternity through the back door. I had a very confused view of God, if I'm being transparent. I'd seen Jesus' Church and how good it could be, and I'd felt Him move around me and do some wonderful things… but I never knew He came to primarily be the bridge for me to walk over to get to the Father.

My friend Tom Allsop often says, 'Revelation minus application equals information, but revelation plus application equals transformation.'[1]

Our problem can be that we know the Bible verses and the stories about what God has done for us, but they are not allowed to sink to the places of our heart where we really need to absorb them. Many of us in the Church have known that God is a father, but not what kind of Father He is. So we hold back. We analyse. We draw our own conclusions as to who He really is, usually based on what we have experienced from our own parents, teachers, authority figures and so on.

The revelation Jesus came to bring is simple: God *is a good Father* (John 17:25-26).

The application is: … *therefore He will father me as His son or daughter* (Romans 8:15).

This may seem basic, but its implications are huge. If we don't see Him as a good father, then we won't let Him father

---

[1] Tom Allsop, pastor, Catch The Fire Three Rivers. Used with permission.

us. If we don't let Him father us, then we remain orphaned in our thinking and in the way we live. Transformation in us and through us is limited or curtailed, and we never get to be the person we were created to be.

Meeting, knowing, walking alongside and living with the Father Jesus came to reveal is our life's goal and our greatest need, whether we realise it or not. It's what we were put on this planet for. When we get it, and start to do it and enjoy it, we actually find it kicks the backside of spiritual orphanness out the door. Knowing who He really is and who we are in Him is the agent of change we need.

The transformation part takes time and it rarely happens without interruptions, distractions or false starts. It does happen, though. Transformation out of orphanness and into sonship and daughterhood happens slowly as we take one step after the other, moving forward on the road alongside Him and towards Him.

The road to the Father's house

So back to my question about this parable of the father and his two sons. Why is it worth our time exploring? I think I wanted some kind of sequel to the Luke 15 story because even as my journey into God's redemption life was beginning, I knew it wasn't going to be a quick one. I knew then, and I know to a much greater degree now, that our intended identities as children of the living God have to be grown into. The revelation of what it looks like, the proof that it's really real and true, and the wonders that come with it all have to be slowly unveiled in our lives through small moments of trust and small choices of faith, as well as those big one-time miracle moments. The unfolding journey of it all builds our faith and trust in God. It builds securely on truth, not feelings or hype. It builds on an unshakable faith that can handle a few storms. Each one of those small steps amounts to part of a long journey towards Him, but also with Him.

This book, these pages, are written to help you not only to find that Father, but also to journey *with* Him and *into* Him. For some, this journey may be for the first time, for others it will be about going deeper and further than you've currently experienced. The more we see of Him the more we find of ourselves. The more our eyes open to all He is, the more we understand who we were made to be. The more we do this, the less we do the prodigal orphan thing. As we'll see, we've all been doing that thing far too long already.

So as we go forward there will be two main areas I'm going to invite you into: a narrative and a personal journey. I encourage you to place yourself in the story that's coming. Be the main character. Have the conversations with God. Make them your own. All of it is written to allow an honest, vulnerable and real conversation with God and your own heart to happen.

I would not presume to invite you to do something I am not doing myself. I've poured as much personal, lived experience into this as I can, and with it as much truth and God words as I can too. Nothing has impacted me more in the last ten years than knowing Him as a father who loves me to my core. Knowing this has meant I've been able to start being the person He always dreamt I could be... and that person is so much better than who I was able to come up with by myself.

I'll be honest. It is not an easy road to walk, this road to the Father's house. I have no intention for you to get to the end of this book and be 'done'. There is no fix that makes the journey unnecessary. All the shortcuts are traps. All of them. There are plenty of places to stop off and pause on the way there that could have you delayed or trapped for decades. It's not a fluffy Christian journey of niceness. It rains on the road, there are potholes and ditches and there are as many overcast, cold days as there are blue-skied ones. The difference is, when walking to the Father's house, you're never on your own, and the One with you is always good and always able.

Our journey of trust and relationship with Him goes on and on throughout our years. God is not only OK with that, it was

His idea that it should be that way. He is invested in our ongoing story of sonship and daughterhood playing out. He knows it will continue to expand and mature long after this book has been put down.

Healthy things grow.

Growing things change.

Healthy change takes time.

Healed-up lives change the world.

Don't be discouraged, it's OK, there's a lot of trust and patience required, but that's the way it's meant to work. The long walk home is worth it in every way imaginable.

My hope and prayer is that you and I, through journeying on the road to the Father's house, will choose to lay down any desire to do it on our own, in our strength or best wisdom. My prayer is that as we go forward we would trust God with our identities and our lives, whatever state we are in. I yearn for us to go deeper in this trust, way deeper than we have ever allowed ourselves to go before.

I truly pray for you as you go on from this point that you would catch the revelation of the son or the daughter that God Himself made you and saved you to be. Adopted and free, healed and whole. Full of life.

2
There's a Path

There's a path, dry and dusty and long, winding over the horizon. Somewhere at the end of this path is a house that belongs to your Father. There was a time when that house used to belong to you, or perhaps, you used to belong to it. This time, though, as you approach, walking that dirt path, you feel like a stranger to it. The silhouette of its shape looks so familiar as it starts to come into view. Memories and images start flashing up as you see its familiar lines against the orange sky. It looks inviting and warm, but you can't help feeling intimidated by its wholeness. You're anything but whole, and this home, this Father's house, just seems to remind you of how far you've fallen.

One step at a time, you draw closer, your feet heavy, but determined. You made up your mind you were coming back. Blisters on your heels and grit under your fingernails. Broken and beaten up by the life that you chose, or perhaps the life someone else chose for you, but you could never let go of. You stumble along, one foot after the other.

Perhaps it wasn't the blisters and bruises for you, perhaps it was the weight of a slowly revealing pride that made these steps so heavy. Life didn't beat you up, it just ignored you – or at least that's how it felt. So you had to make something for yourself. You got by. You learned to scoff at dreamers and idealists because they just hadn't been dealt the hand you had yet. That kind of thinking helped, but it also got you tired and got you lonely.

Each step towards the house is taking you away from the former life you lived, but the marks of that life are still on your body and in your eyes. You know the story you've lived. Luke 15, the prodigal son, the proud son – whatever you want to call it, it's a tale you've become very familiar with over the years. Living with the consequences of those choices of pride and independence is what ultimately brought you to this path. Now you are simply stumbling towards hope. Stumbling towards your Father's house.

Looking back now, you can say finding yourself on that road was the best place you could ever be. You remember, like it was yesterday, when you were 'still a long way off', when He entered the scene.

Dad.

Not earthly dad. Not surrogate dad. Not father figure. Not 'like a father to me'. But Abba. Daddy.

Father God.

A Father who made up His mind a long time ago that He would contend for you on your worst day.

You think back to what it felt like to be rugby-tackled by this Dad on that path, thrown to the ground, not to be beaten or punished for the messes and mistakes… but covered instead with kisses and squeezed with the most loving embrace you've ever felt. A collision. All your brokenness with all His grace. The tears and the snot. The ring. The cloak. The dancing brilliance in your Dad's eyes.

Instantaneous forgiveness.

Right now, you can recall that exact moment in your mind's eye. I say 'exact moment' knowing that it could have been one moment in a ministry line or several hundred moments spread over months or years when you felt that fatherly affection pressing in on you. Whatever form it took, you remember it as a collision with grace. Every fear you had and every ounce of shame was overcome by the love of God. You remember being picked up, feeling the strong arm of the Father lifting your weak limbs and placing you on your feet again.

You were on a dirt path, stumbling towards hope… and then suddenly you weren't. You left the path, clothed and covered, that ring glinting in the sunlight on your finger; those ruined sandals that you used to cling to left forgotten and discarded in a ditch as you stepped forward in those new leather soles. And step by step you got closer and closer until the silhouette of that house, Dad's house, suddenly burst into warm, welcoming colours. It looked just as you remembered it did, but now it had the air of invitation and welcome in a way that you never appreciated.

You walked up the steps to the front door, pulled forward the handle and entered into the wildest party celebration you've seen. You were hugged by everyone, some people you remembered, some you'd never met but they seemed to know you, and everywhere you looked you saw the genuine sparkle in the eyes looking back at you, none brighter than your Daddy's as He looked at you. You filled your plate and stuffed yourself. All of it was grace and goodness and life. And at the end of the evening you just lay at your Dad's feet, knowing you were home.

Lying curled up in bed later that evening, you wondered, quietly, what you were going to do with this life you'd now been gifted with. You'd become an expert in everything required to live outside this house, on your own, relying on no one but yourself, a spiritual orphan's lot. But now all those strategies and techniques to live by were just waiting to be deleted. They were not going to be useful in the days to come. They were going to be dead weights. They needed to go.

And as you thought about all the ways you learned to cope, your mind flowed over all the false comforts, all the self-soothing behaviour, all the pride and all the crud that caused you to leave this house in the first place.

Is everything that pulled you away from the Father's house now gone? Has the fear been eradicated? The shame wiped from your memory banks? What of pride and self-assurance… are they still in there somewhere? Is sin now a thing of the past?

'To what degree am I truly free? To what degree am I loosened from those cords? Did I leave all my chains on that dirt road?'

You didn't ponder these things for much longer. You were tired and full with all the love and comfort of being home, back in your Father's home; it was just too overwhelming for any anxious thoughts to penetrate. And so you drifted off and slept as a redeemed and rescued child of God.

Because that is what you were.

A couple of days later, maybe weeks, you choose to go and take a walk back to that old dirt path. Ring on your finger, cloak still around you, new shoes still fitting firm. You find yourself trying to find the spot where the grace collision happened. And your mind starts thinking about what stewarding this gift of restoration is going to look like. How much are you going to choose to embrace the freedom? How deeply are you going to trust?

What happens when the thing that scared you the most, that addiction you leaned on the longest, the shame you've run from and hidden in the deepest parts of you... what happens if it rears its head and comes back? You hate even thinking this way – you know God is good. But there's still something niggling.

It seems fear, shame, control and anxiety still have some place of occupancy in you.

You look down the way, at the paths going away from the Father's house; you remember where they lead and what kind of houses await at the end of them.

Here's the thing – the question you're pondering as you stand there is not, 'Have I been truly restored?', the question is, 'Do I know what it means to live in the Father's house as a son, as a daughter?'

When grace collided with you on that dirt path, it wasn't just to rescue or restore you. It was to invite you, and me – and everyone who gets to experience that moment – into something new. It was to invite us to dwell in a place Jesus said had been set apart of us to live in.[2] To thrive in. To expand in. A place where we would be under the same roof as the Father, Son and Holy Spirit.

You stand on the pathway where the moment of your redemption happened, and your mind swims with all these thoughts. What you choose to do from this moment on is entirely up to you.

Many down the years have made it their mission to live in the post-prodigal house flawlessly, not putting one step out of place. They got rescued by love, but their effort, their gifting and their devotion is going

2 John 14:2.

to be the fruit of that saving. For them that effort is going to be the equity that keeps them in the good books.

Some have stumbled away from the house back to the path, in the process falling into ditches and scraping their knees. Then returning to the Father's house they live desperately trying to cover up every cut and scrape so no one will see the poor way they've really handled His gift.

Many others don't even make it to the porch. They get partway back and then wander completely off the path and into the tall grass, never finding their way home, turning their back on His house forever.

And many, so many, just camp by the banks of the dirt path, maybe within eyeshot of the house… but never entering it. Too afraid. Too uncertain. Too wary. Life spent watching other stumblers, and the striders, making their way home is seemingly more preferable to them.

The sun is almost fully risen. You're not them, you're you. So, decision-making time.

What kind of son, what kind of daughter, are you going to choose to be?

Are you going to see Him as He is, and yourself as He intended?

Or do you have another plan…?

How's that been working out for you?

I find myself understanding the things of the kingdom by analogies and metaphors. I think I would have been the person following Jesus who breathed a sigh of relief every time He spoke using a parable. There is something about the story, the simile and the allegory that just helps my brain understand much bigger concepts. I did a theology degree and studied Christology, systematic theology, biblical Greek, you name it. But I'd still 100 per cent be the guy thanking Jesus for putting it all in simple-to-follow story form.

Simple stories have taught me deep truths that my intellect would take years to grasp. As a child growing up in the 1980s and 90s, there was no shortage of 'good vs evil' cartoons and movies. I genuinely think I first truly understood what sacrifice was from watching *Transformers: The Movie*, watching the great

Optimus Prime lay his life down for his fellow robot people. I didn't want Bambi as a child, it was robots for me. As I grew up I started getting the concept of the Father heart of God from characters like Mufasa in *The Lion King*. The years passed and it was *The Lord of the Rings* films that unveiled how hope, even if it was weak and fragile, really could avail itself against evil. Most recently the TV show *The Chosen* has shown me that Jesus may actually have had a really good sense of humour, that people may have gathered around Him because He made them feel alive.

All of this is to say, imagery helps me see and understand things I intellectually would have trouble with, and I don't think I'm alone with that. Storytelling has always been God's way of helping humankind to remember important truths. I was made with a desire to see the visual God, the One who loves to use what He's made to point to Himself. I like that.

When I look at the story in Luke 15 of the prodigal son I see the whole thing playing out in my mind like a film, and one of the first things I go to in my head is location; where the sons and the Father are as the story unfolds.

There's a path, a house and, connecting them both, a road.

I think the path leads to a lot of places. It goes two ways for a start: towards home and away from it. It can lead you into hope and it can take you away from it. If you were paying attention to your feet, you would see that the further away from home you got the more broken the path became. If you were on your way towards your home, you'd see the path beneath you turn from dirt to stone and then eventually to gold.

I think the path led the younger son to the far-off land where he messed his life up and lost his way. I think the same path led the older brother out to some fields where he made up his mind to live his life based on a 'you reap what you sow' mentality.[3]

I've been on paths like that before. You walk down them, talking to yourself, muttering and mumbling and trying to come

---

[3] Galatians 6:7-9, Luke 15:27-30.

up with the right line or piece of dialogue that will appease God or get you out of the trouble you got yourself into. Sometimes it's more selfish than that. Sometimes it's the place where you justify to yourself all the ways in which you were right and everyone else was wrong. All the best lines you should have or could have said seem to come to mind when you walk down the path.

I'd say the path for some is a place where people walk with their heads down in shame or defeat, where every stone and exposed tree root seems to cause further stumbling. There are trenches, ditches and potholes that seem to swallow people alive for decades. For others I'd say the path is a place where people walk with their heads held high in pride or overconfidence. They look impressive but I don't know how many of them are aware of just how far from home they are wandering. I think some people spend their entire lives wandering back and forth on the path, always moving, never arriving anywhere.

I don't think the path is necessarily a bad place, I just think it is walked by the broken and the hurting. It is not an evil place, it has just known a lot of hurting people walk it. The path is where we find ourselves when we realise we're not where we should be. The broken paths we've walked down can be redeemed. They can become the way back home for us and for others; they can be the evidence of God's grace in our life, the source of hope for other wandering and lost people.

So, there's a path, but there's also a house. The house is a good place. The house is where the Father lives. The house is where we're all meant to live. It's where the 'spirit part of us' in those 'heavenly places'[4] starts unpacking its bags and gets settled in the moment we get saved, long before the rest of us catches up. I believe the house is the place where the fragile things of our hearts that need kindness and restoration are attended to. It's also the place where ideas that will transform the world find their origin. The Father's house is a safe roof over your head

---

[4] Ephesians 2:6.

and mine. It's a place of abundant resources. I think it has more rooms than it looks like it should have from the outside. It think it just keeps going the deeper into it you go. Physically as a space it doesn't really make any sense, both small and intimate, but also bigger than the universe as we know it.

The Father's house is the home our hearts and souls have always wanted.

Now, I'd love to say when we get saved and made new in God we just get transported up off the path of worldly things and deposited in this house where somehow everything just kind of works out for us all the time. No hassle. No struggle. Certainly no situations where things looked like they were going to work out and then didn't. No times when someone who gets prayer for healing doesn't get the miracle we were all believing for.

Although that sounds appealing, it is unfortunately not biblically or experientially accurate. To believe that would be to essentially believe that the moment we get saved and become a Jesus follower we get raptured and placed in heaven right in that exact moment. Clearly that is not what happens, nor is it God's plan for us in this life. Yes, the house is heaven, but it's also a place of identity and resourcing that can be lived in now and today. The house is for now and it is to come. We'll get into that in the next chapter.

So, a path and a house.

What connects the path and the house is a road.

This is the road the son and his dad in the parable walked back on.

It's not a dirt path or one made of sand with rocky and muddy patches; it's solid. There are trenches either side of it and you don't want to fall in them – but it's a solid and dependable road, and it will get you to where you need to go. With a good guide, you'll never put a foot wrong.

Picture this. Brick and smooth cobbled stone, warm to the touch. The more you walk it the more intricate it gets, the more refined the stones become, the more secure your feet feel. After a while of walking on this road, you could swear the stones beneath your feet look like gold and precious stones. We're talking about the King's road here. The road that leads to the Father's mansion, the palace, the safest place, the temple, the engine factory of the universe and source of the river of God that flows out to bring healing to all the nations.[5]

The road to the Father's house is, essentially, where our life journey with God and towards Him should happen. It's where all our days and months and decades were intended to unfold. Now, if we choose to stand still, do things our own way, trust in culture's wisdom and the ever-revolving door of what passes as truth in our current times, then we choose the broken path. If we choose to take small, simple, even stumbling steps of trust towards God, well, then we start walking on the road to the Father's house. In this story, using this imagery, it really is as simple as those two choices.

We have to be authentic here; walking the road isn't the easy option. It is often not pretty and it can be painful. The reward can seem so distant at times that our heart can go through seasons of wrestling with each step we try to take. Despite this, the road really is the good choice and the wise choice. The more we walk it, the more we find others walking it too, all desiring to get to the Father's house. The encouragement you get from these people might just provide some of the best memories and moments of your life. The walking of it together can be so glorious and so wondrous that there are times when you can't believe that it is you getting to live this life and seeing these miraculous moves of God.

So, a path and a house, and a road connecting the two.

These are our choices.

Remember, like any journey, you can go both ways. You can travel to the Father's house or away from it.

---

[5] Revelation 22:2.

The person we believe ourselves to be and choices and agreements we make as a result of that will determine which direction we go in.

Five-year-old theology

It seems like a no-brainer, surely, that the steps we should take are ones that get us closer to the Father's house, not further away. So why isn't everyone doing it? The reason has a lot to do with how we see ourselves and how we see the Father.

It's somewhere around 1988 and I'm about five years old, give or take. The BBC has started broadcasting its version of The Chronicles of Narnia, *The Lion, the Witch and the Wardrobe*, as a weekly show. I've never seen it before and so every episode is undoing my little mind and heart. Peter, Susan, Edmund and Lucy entering through the wardrobe into the magical land of Narnia. Edmund's temptation by the White Witch, his rescue, Aslan the great Lion sacrificing himself on the stone table, his resurrection – all of it just blew me away.

The Narnia story kindled my love of imaginary worlds and storytelling. It showed me that the most powerful truths can be conveyed in allegories simple enough for a child to understand. You can see where the path and the house come from in my head now.

About the same time, I think I heard the parable of the prodigal son for the first time. I was just about old enough to pay attention in church or at my school's weekly Mass, and a Bible story was always shared there.

Somewhere in my mind I made a pairing of these two stories that would stick with me for a long time to come. Sat in front of our electric fire at home, watching another episode of C S Lewis' story, this is what I was thinking: 'Peter was the strong leader. Susan seemed so confident. Little Lucy just seemed so innocent and yet so courageous and trusting. And Edmund... well, he's just the prodigal son of the whole tale.'

Now, if you haven't read *The Lion, the Witch and the Wardrobe*,[6] I may have lost you there. I'm going to assume that most people have, or at least have seen the movie. Edmund lets himself down and also his family. He is part of a family and has a great destiny ahead of him, yet he makes a deal with the devil to get pleasure, a selfish need met, and he hurts himself and so many others in the process.

The prodigal son did the same thing. He sold his sonship for a piece of supposed freedom and then paid the price for his choice. Both of them had all they needed already, they just couldn't see it.

There's a point here we would do well to pause on for a moment. You can have your true identity spoken of and even affirmed, yet if it has not sunk in to you, then you are completely capable and perhaps even likely to make 'the orphan-hearted choice' when opportunity comes knocking. The son in Luke 15 knew the father, knew his home, knew that he belonged to something greater than himself, but like Edmund, he didn't know it in his heart. He chose to put aside his identity, who he really was as a son of the house, and instead he chose to embrace independence.

There was no big signpost saying 'make this choice and you will be acting like a spiritual orphan'. It never works like that. He just stopped being a true son of his father, he stepped outside the covering, and when you do that, you're really just stepping into the orphan thing. It's very easy when you are in that place to forget who you are and spend your life grasping for whatever it is you can get.

The prodigal's choice led him miles away from his father's house, eventually to be penniless, isolated and up to his elbows in pig filth. Edmund in his story didn't do much better.

Now, I don't think my five-year-old brain was theologically trying to come up with allegories and spiritual similes to make

<hr>

[6] C S Lewis, *The Lion, the Witch, and the Wardrobe* (London: Geoffrey Bles, 1950).

sense of all this; I wasn't trying to tie together C S Lewis' tale with Jesus' parable for a good sermon illustration. My greatest academic challenge at this point in my life was learning how to write the number 2 correctly. I just know my heart was trying to make sense of the emotions that were bubbling up as I saw these stories unfold. A basic, childlike understanding of what 'choices' could lead to was forming inside me and I was starting to understand that it was possible to make a choice that would lead to me growing into the best version of me, or to sink down into something less or something worse.

Both of these stories portray the brokenness of a human who has forgotten who they are. Both stories involve a child being rescued while still in their shame and in their chains. Both stories involve an unfair solution weighted in favour of the perpetrator and the sinner. Edmund restored to his place as a prince and future king, his life debt paid by another. The younger son restored to his place as son of the father, his shame covered by his dad.

As I looked at these stories as a child, I felt something that only my adult brain can now start to put language to. Like the prodigal, I too get to see the fierce compassion of Father God running towards me, on my lowest day. We meet, me battered and bruised, Him whole and overwhelmingly good and free, and in that moment my greatest hope is realised...

God is good.

And He is not repelled by me.

The Luke 15 parable Jesus tells about His Father and ours tells of a dad falling on his son with kisses, taking him off the path and covering over every sign that his child had lived rough and beaten down. He restores his identity and his position and celebrates him with the biggest party of the year. This is God. This is our Lord. This is what He is like and has always been like.

The Father Jesus tells us about is the God of Abraham, Isaac and Jacob.[7] He's the Hebrew God. The Old Testament God. He didn't just become a nice God or a good Father in the New Testament. The Bible isn't retconning the character of God – He has always been this way. Jesus is simply revealing something that was always true, it had just been misplaced.

As I watch this tale play out, all my misunderstandings, theories and fears of God the Father being a bully, a punitive taskmaster or reluctant creator are obliterated by this truth.

How can He be disgusted with me when He's hugging the hell out of me?

How can He be repulsed by the stench of my sin when He leans into me rather than away?

How can I feel shame about how low I have fallen when His knees are pressed into the dirt of the same path I have fallen down on?

How can I not trust Him when He puts himself through shame to get to me?

When I think of how great the cost of my sin is, He stands up from the table having already cleared the cheque when my back was turned.

The Father's redemption dealt with the past, but it was not just an act affecting the past. The parable shows us that we have been saved from something and saved to something. There is an equal emphasis both on what the sons were being saved from, the sin and pride and independence, and on what they now had the opportunity to step into as truly restored and rehabilitated sons.

Just as in his story, Edmund, the traitor, is rescued and redeemed so that he can be a king, in the parable the two sons are invited to step out of their chosen orphanness and back into being sons of the Father, with all the rights and privileges that entails.

---

[7] See Exodus 3:6.

Put simply, what is being revealed to us here is the overwhelming kindness of God as He meets us on the dirt floor in all our mess. The simple outcome of all this is that He rekindles our hope for the life He intended for us to live.

A life of forgiveness.

A life of restoration.

A chance to start again.

A chance to dream again.

An invitation to come back home.

Coming off the path

Many of us want to get off the path of our brokenness and embrace this life of forgiveness and restoration. We want to be done with the pain and the coping strategies of the orphan life and have that fresh start as a child of God. We may have enjoyed the buzz of whatever our chosen addictive outlets were for a time, but we know there is no future in them. The drink, the porn, the food, being seen and loved by the crowd, or maybe just the feelings of control we had have shown themselves for what they are. They are not our future. In our hearts God put a longing to be on a secure and solid road to somewhere good. The problem is, none of us is going to step off the familiar path we've been walking and onto the road to the Father's house if inside us we don't believe God is good. We just won't do it.

You can reread the last few pages as much as you like and take in all the good things said about who the Father is and what is in His heart for us His children, but if you don't believe it you'll stay exactly where you are. You'll never go within 100 miles of that road if you only see an angry, disappointed, demanding father waiting at the end of it.

Being told about how nice and wonderful someone is, is one thing. Many people have been told God is good and nice, but have not experienced Him for themselves.

What they have experienced, however, is examples of abusive or absent fathers, performance-orientated leaders, pastors expecting perfection, or teachers and bosses expecting results, all of which have a huge and dramatic effect in shaping us. When we think of 'the Father' we think of one of those people, their words or their expectations, each one becoming a filter over our eyes until the real Father is blocked from view or twisted and bent out of shape.

It is time to start taking these filters off.

If a plant is never watered, it will have no chance of growing; likewise, we will not be able to grow in anything or in any direction of calling, relationships or dreams if we don't have the goodness of God watering our lives. You can run a small group, preach, be the youth leader or the missions pastor and you can have the best marketplace business or happiest family unit and *still doubt* that God is good and for you.

The Father *is* a good Father. The Dad who comes out to find us on the path and bring us home can be trusted. He does it all for our restoration, not for our punishment. Yes, He knows all we have done and thought and all the ways we have got it wrong. He loves us all the same, regardless. He is not the father who demanded too much from you or had no time for you. He is not the pastor who was too busy for you or the school teacher who was always suspicious of you. He is the good Father. He will always have time for you. He formed you, your heart, your spine, the splash of colours in your eyes and the complexities of your brain and your heart. He made us unique and said we were good.

The filthy and exhausted son on the path needed to *re-meet* his father. He needed to put aside what he thought he knew about him to find out who he really was. In finding him he ended up finding himself. It will be the same for us when we are able to start trusting that the Father is exactly who Jesus says He is.

We all have filters over our eyes that affect how we see the Father. Some will have been put there by other people; some we may have allowed to be put in place; others, we may have no idea where they came from. I'd like to invite you to take a step forward towards the Father's house and trust that He is who He says He is. What do I mean by that? Between you and God, away from the eyes of others or the pressure of trying to do it 'the right religious way', ask Him to remove those filters by which you've been seeing Him. Pray it simply, like a child would ask their dad for something, knowing that the One you're asking wants the best for you and is able.

Some of the people who helped create those filters in the first place will need to be forgiven and released from your heart judgements.

You will probably need to forgive yourself too. I used to think it was just about me repenting of all my mistakes; turns out I was holding myself in unforgiveness and needed to let myself out of jail. Just remember that forgiving someone doesn't mean that what was done to you was OK or excusable, it just means you're taking the person who did it to you out of a headlock, and giving them back to God.

These steps aren't necessarily easy, but we can do them when we start believing, with childlike faith, that God is good, just and full of mercy and grace and is going to help us.

When we begin to do that, our hearts forget what we thought we knew about Him. We start to believe He's a good Father who wants to bring us safely home. And so we let Him pull us up off that dirt path, set us on our feet and start the journey home, side by side with Him.

3
Things That Were Once Lost

Sometimes you wish you had a better memory.

It's not that you're forgetting things, it's just that some experiences can happen in such a blur that trying to remember them and pick out the individual moments isn't always easy.

The walk back to the house with your Dad is one of those moments.

There was so much going on inside your heart and your head that untangling it now feels like trying to lay straight last year's Christmas lights after they had been stuffed unceremoniously into a box once the tree came down. Impossible.

You weren't expecting the forgiveness. Not in the way it came. No way.

To be honest, when you saw your Dad running towards you, that look of fierce determination in His eyes, you thought punishment was coming. Actions have consequences. You know that. Fathers discipline their children with punishment, with abandonment, with lessons that need learning... that's the world; you know that, right? When the kisses and the laughter and the squeeze of His hug came, well, it was shocking. You were simply unprepared for it.

It was so unexpected. So overwhelming. So public. So lavish. So unrelenting. Your speech, with all its logical reasoning about where you should go and what you should do now you'd dragged yourself home, was simply brushed aside and ignored.

You weren't expecting any of this.

So it's no wonder your mind was swimming as you started that walk back to the house. You do remember that you talked together. Your Dad asked how you were. He looked at some cuts on your arm, a bottle of ice-cold water appeared from somewhere – that was very welcome. You and your Dad just kept on walking and talking. The path beneath your feet started to level out.

He just wanted to hear your voice.

You didn't know what to say. How do you share what you've been up to when most of it was sin and rebellion and selfish independence?

He didn't seem to have the same embarrassment or awkwardness that you had. He just listened and smiled and never once took His arm off your shoulder.

You don't remember all of it, but you're pretty sure when you shared the worst of it… you were held more tightly.

The whole of Luke 15 is about lost things being contended for, sought out and found.

There are three stories Jesus tells in the chapter. In fact, the entire chapter is these stories, one after the other, progressing one into the next. Each story is about a lost thing. A sheep, a coin and a son. Three lost things. Each story has people searching and each story has the searchers experiencing the same ending.

The first story is about a shepherd (vv4-7). He's caring for a flock of a hundred and one of them goes missing. One of his own sheep, lost, gone, unaccounted for. He goes searching day and night, traversing terrain and searching unceasingly until he finds that sheep. Caught in a thicket or with its head through a fence… who knows. It needed rescuing and its master sought it out and didn't stop until he'd found it.

I haven't lost a sheep, so I don't have a story about that, unfortunately. I do, however, know what it's like being a school teacher taking a class of thirty schoolchildren on a trip out and trying to get them home in one piece. A couple of times a year in my former life as a teacher I would lead a field trip somewhere, and every time I took my class on one of these trips, paranoid thoughts would fly through my mind at random intervals. I would stop every five minutes to do a headcount, double and triple check after the kids took a toilet visit, you name it. It's a never-relenting tension that is present for the whole day. I know what it's like to get to twenty-nine children in the headcount and then be one shy. The pit of my stomach would fall out. Suddenly your entire world is about finding that one missing child.

Usually they were in the toilets, but that's beside the point. When you know you have a flock and one of them goes missing, they become the most important thing in your life. That's how the shepherd felt about the one missing sheep from his flock.

The story of the shepherd is followed by a story of a woman looking for a lost coin. In verse 8 of Luke 15 Jesus tells us that she searches everywhere trying to find it. Up all night, looking for a single coin. She loses sleep for this thing; it's that important to her.

Once when I was in school, on a particularly hot summer day, I sold a 10p ice lolly to a boy in the class below me for £1. It had been the last lolly in the freezer of the shop near our school. We were all standing outside school waiting for our mums to come and this one kid, a few years younger than me, was so desperate for an ice lolly he was willing to pay me well over the odds for it. I felt a little bad selling it to him at such an extortionate price, but I wasn't as versed in generosity as I am now. I've got to be honest, it was one of the shrewdest financial moves I'd made in my eight years of being alive.

What I can tell you, however, is that if I had lost that £1 I gained from him I would have been up all night looking for it. It was that much of a prize and trophy to me. You could buy a lot of sweets and chocolate for £1 back in the 1990s. Like the woman, the moment I found it I would have called up my friends and had a serious celebration. I get where that woman was at.

So a missing sheep from the flock and a valuable coin missing and then a story of two sons and one incredible father. This story is about a father who goes out to his sons, both lost in their own ways, and offers them a lifeboat.

The shepherd searching for the lost sheep, the woman searching for the lost coin, and then the father looking for his lost sons.

Tom Allsop puts it this way: 'The coin doesn't know it's lost. The sheep knows it's lost but doesn't know the way home. The son knows he's lost and knows the way home but has to decide to turn and go home.'[8]

I think that's a pretty good summary.

We aren't the best experts on how we are doing or even where we are. We don't know when we're lost half the time. We think we're OK or just trying to make it through a difficult season. Seasons have beginnings and ends, yet we just throw the word 'season' out as a catch-all definer of what we seem to be in but can't fully rationalise.

The Father is the One who owns us, the One who protects us, the One who birthed us and the One who knows just how well we're doing. He is the One who knows just how found or lost we are. He knows just how settled or anxious we are in our hearts, or how fragile we are. He knows when hope is within us and when it isn't.

The Father knows what to do in all of these cases.

He knows how to rescue things that are lost and don't know it.

He knows how to save people who know they are lost but don't know the way home.

He knows how to redeem people who know they are lost and know the way home, but can't do it by themselves.

I was the last of these. The boy who knew he was lost and knew the way home but was too scared and intimidated to take it. I think it was shame that held me back more than anything.

---

[8] Tom Allsop, 2013. Used with permission.

One out of a hundred sheep, one out of ten coins, one out of two sons. You and I are valuable to the Father. The image of God is all over and within us. Like the coin Jesus held up to the religious questioners, stamped with the image of Caesar,[9] God holds you and me in His hands, stamped with His image.[10] This is where our value originates. This is what makes you and me worth searching for.

The longest journey (the real one)

I used to have a full head of hair. Then I became a school teacher and in the space of about five years a full-on receding retreat took place. I don't know if the two were connected, but it's hard not to see the link. Don't get me wrong, I loved my job, I loved the madness of a school day, I loved the children, and the weird and profound things that would come out of their mouths on a regular basis. But the one thing that would regularly rob me of my peace, and then set fire to it, was a familiar scenario when the children and I would revisit or recap some school subject we had looked at very recently:

> 'OK, everyone, long division, we did this yesterday…
> who can tell me the four steps we learned?'
> Silence.
> 'OK, who can tell me one of the steps… just one
> of them…?'
> Nothing but a painful uncomfortable silence only
> punctuated by a ticking clock.
> 'OK, let's take it down a notch. What are we doing
> when we divide something?'
> My hand gestures are becoming wildly over
> exaggerated as I try to show them as much of the
> answer as I can without just giving the whole thing

---

9 Matthew 22:19-21.
10 Genesis 1:27.

away. Still nothing. I'm now at my last throw of the dice.

'When we divide something, are we making it bigger... or smaller?'

The children were six years old. I knew they were young but the only person with their hand up was the one girl who always knows the answer to every question, and I was really trying to avoid asking her just on principle.

With a slightly resigned tone I quietly conceded and went back to basics.

'OK, who remembers we were even doing maths yesterday...?'

Making progress one day and then seeing it all virtually disappear overnight was hard to ignore. I think the problem was that my expectations were too high. I was regularly creating a situation where, in the midst of a whole day of experiences, input, trials, traumas and triumphs in these six-year-olds' lives, they were having a grown-up demand that they remember and recite something specific they had heard twenty-four hours previously. In the midst of all the inputs their brains were receiving and trying to process, they were unable to retain something that would really help them.

You and I may not be children, but the influx of inputs into our lives is no different from what those children were experiencing. Culture, media, family, finances, emails and entertainment all do their job in crowding what is going on inside our heads. All important. All demanding.

If you're a Christian and have been a member of a church, you're going to have heard a lot of sermons. You'll have heard lots of preachers standing up and saying, 'What I'm speaking on today really is the most important thing in the kingdom,' or words to that effect. You'll have sung a lot of songs, read a lot of blogs, books, posts and probably more memes than you can count. You maybe follow a couple of solid Christian leaders on social media, or maybe you're reading that book everyone is raving about, every night before bed. I'm not being cynical about those things, but that can be life for a Christian, right?

You and I have got stuff coming at us and into us almost constantly. So much good, so much average and so much *whatever*. And like the sower sowing his seed in the field (Matthew 13), some of it takes, some of it doesn't and quite a lot of it gets swallowed up by something else and never fruits in the way that you hoped it would. All of it pulls and tugs at our souls within us; like a boat on the waves, our soul feels and experiences all of it.

You've probably heard it said that the longest journey you'll ever take is from your head to your heart. There's an awful lot of truth in that. The things we think we know about God and ourselves in our heads take on a whole new level of profound life-changing revelation when they migrate to our hearts. Stuff starts changing when truth hits our hearts. It takes a long time to believe something you know. Now, although this statement is true, I think you and I are probably experiencing a more acute one that beats it to first place.

The longest journey is from the spirit to the soul.

Your spirit is 'seated … in the heavenly places' and it is complete in Jesus; Ephesians 2:6 tells us that. What does this mean? One meaning is that in the spiritual realm – the heavenlies, that place we occasionally glimpse, that place that is full of activity – our spirits dwell with God there. When we allow ourselves to be led by our spirit we become fearless in the kingdom. We start praying prayers that we would never have dared to pray before because they would have just sounded like madness. We start believing for things we never would have dared to believe.

I prayed for a man once who had limped to church that morning having not been able to come for months because of the searing pain in his leg. When I saw him I just knew that God had something for him that day, that he wasn't going to leave empty-handed. In my heart the familiar old lies and intimations had already started: 'Wait for a more senior leader… just bless him, don't expect it to actually heal… this isn't going to happen so don't even bother.'

My soul had seen and experienced disappointment in prayer before; it had plenty of ammunition for insecurity about praying for miracles. Now, unfortunately for the lies and the insecurities, I had already made the decision to trust that God could do supernatural miracles through Alistair Forman just as He could through any other person. I knew that underneath those choppy soul waters there was a calm in my spirit. I knew God could do this, I didn't know that He *would*, but I believed He *could* use me and that He wants heaven on earth, wholeness in the place of brokenness. There's no sickness in heaven and so that was all I needed in the moment to dive head first in to praying for this guy's leg.

We prayed, he tested it and suddenly it started to bend without pain. This guy wasn't faking anything. He was twice my age and tears were streaming down his face as he held his arms up in the air, praising God for what was happening. I tried to hug him to celebrate but he didn't hug me back, he was too enthralled with standing tall and thanking God to notice me any more.

Moments like that can happen when we let our spirits lead; when they are anchored to God, waves and storms don't affect them. When Paul writes in Ephesians about how we are seated with God, he uses the aorist tense; this is a tense he uses in other portions of Scripture, such as Romans 8:30 when he talks of how we have been 'glorified' and Colossians 3:1 when he says we have been 'raised with Christ'. The aorist tense is used when something has *already happened.* It's a fact, a done deal, something that is not in dispute. So the raising, being seated, being glorified, all of it is past tense fact. It's happened. It is part of the being and new nature of a believer.

The spirit part of us gets this and lives from that truth.

Our souls, the rest of us? Well, that's very much still figuring it all out. It is experiencing the world that is constantly in transition. The soul and body part of us is playing a game of catch-up to something that's already happened to our spirit. Like the children in my class, it needs reminding almost daily of what was learned the day before.

Our soul knows we have been changed and it knows a profound transition is underway (sanctification) but it finds it so hard to fall in line. It's been too conditioned, too moulded by events and time. It's had people speak into it and tell it how to act and how to feel for years. It has habits and patterns. It has expectations for trouble and wariness from false hopes and it's probably forgotten just how much delight can be found in God and in the gift of life in Him.

For some of us, our souls have been violated and taken advantage of. Great violence may have been perpetrated against your soul and it has ever since defended itself and set up protective walls to make sure it never happens again.

If you are a believer in Jesus, then a supernatural renewal has happened in your life. A done deal. A transformation has occurred. Your spirit felt it when the Father embraced you on that road, when the Son covered you and the Spirit filled you, *but it will take a lifetime* to seep its way into the deepest recesses of your soul. The soul will need a type of long-term immersion in this renewal to feel the change. If you're not a believer in Jesus, then everything is being led by your soul; it's all you've got, but it doesn't need to be.

In so many ways too numerous to mention here, I know that my soul can still act like that kid on the path. It's still thinking on and operating from so many of the things that took me down that path in the first place. It still gets hurt the way it got hurt. It still gets scared the way it got scared. It's not that I doubt that any of the breakthrough I received actually happened – I know it happened – it's just that I am coming to realise that only parts of me have *actually got it*.

The Father wants *all of us* to get it, to realise just how restored and renewed we are. In the next section, we're going to look at one of the most common reasons we struggle with doing this.

You don't live there any more

Let's do some foundational stuff quickly so we can start to untangle some of the questions that are arising.

If you have given up on trying to fix your life, repented for all the independence and all the sin and accepted Jesus as your personal Saviour, Lord and best friend, *then you're not a prodigal any more.*

Just take a moment on that one.

You're not a prodigal in His eyes any more.

You're not walking the identity path of a spiritual orphan any more.

You're not on your own, fighting for your own place in the world any more.

Deep breath in and out. Let that one settle.

You know that something changed when you became a Jesus follower. That old shack that your spirit person dwelt in got bulldozed. The camping gear you clung to as you drifted from one place to the next has gone in the trash. The palace you'd retreat to, to hide behind piles of money, has had its lock changed. Those places are no longer your home. Your home is the Father's house. The post-prodigal house. The journey to being a son or daughter of God, who is no longer held by fear, no longer crippled by addiction, obsessed with sin management or unable to step out of the boat into calling is the journey you are now on.

You're both living in the house... and you're making your way to it.

It's the now and not-yet kingdom.

Many Christians labour under the belief that we are only technically redeemed, but not in any practically felt way. We start to experience the joy of having a spirit that has been brought alive by God's grace, but our souls still feel so buried in the old life we used to live. All our habits and practices are so wrapped up with what we used to do and how we used to live.

Grace gloriously interrupts our analysing, though. Our ways of thinking can one day be God's greatest gift to us and other days be our biggest stumbling block. Our minds start to be renewed (Romans 12:2) once we have that grace collision with God. That grace starts trickling in to help us think differently, and the old identity statement of 'I'm a fundamentally bad person who occasionally does good things' gets exposed as the lie that it is in the Father's house.

However, the renewing of the mind can feel slow at times. *Painfully slow*, almost to the degree that you're not even sure if you've changed at all. That's why it's so important to have good people in your life who can remind you that you are a son or daughter who lives in and from the Father's house, not a prodigal on the road. These people will also be better at pointing out when and where you have made progress than you are. For every moment you feel you haven't changed, they will remind you that Jesus saved you, the Father is fathering you and the Spirit of God is dwelling in you. We need people like this in our lives; the company we keep is so hugely important. It's clichéd but there's a reason for that. Sons and daughters in the kingdom need brothers and sisters who will speak to who they really are, not to the mask or the façade that they present, nor from the perspective of the culture around them.

Now, I'm not suggesting that we hide away from people who think 'in worldly ways' and go and live in some kind of pre-apocalyptic commune, cut off from the rest of humanity. The point here isn't 'be around *more* Christian people', it is 'be around people who know who God truly is and who they are in Him'.

Around the world, churches are full of people waiting for heaven, hoping to just make it across the finish line. No big dreams in God. No expectation of the abundance of heaven or a lavish answer to a prayer. No sense of how much they are loved. No revelation that their heavenly Father is different from their earthly father and mother – that kind of life doesn't need to be our kind of life any more.

For too long I was this Christian. I was this believer. Totally unaware that the dirt path I had been rescued from was no longer my home or my inheritance.

I was a son of God on paper, but in reality I was living like an orphan. I was filled with His Spirit but living as if I was empty. Somehow living life on the path and all it offered was the best I had come to expect. I was trying to do some good where I went, and I know I did a lot of good for God and for people. But I was also a steaming hot mess.

This is not the kind of life the Father pulled me off the path to live. It doesn't need to be the kind of life you live, either. A life full of mental pressure and anxiety that you are messing up God's gracious gift is not what He won for you. A day-to-day existence of trying to impress God or people with your efforts and your success is not what Jesus hung on the cross for.

Real, full and true life was won for me and for you and given as a free gift of grace. When we try to somehow sustain this gift by our hard work, we miss the point of the gift. The Galatians got it in the neck when Paul wrote to them about this.[11]

You and I have had our home address altered. It now reads 'The Father's House'. That's where our mail goes. That's where our bills get sent. That's where the only mirrors we ever look in reside. That's where we return after a bad day at work. That's where we go to renew and recover. His house is our house. It's a place where only sons and daughters live. All orphans are welcome, but the moment they truly step over the threshold of repentance and acceptance, they cease to be lost and become found children of God with their own room in His home.

That is where we now live.

The goal is not, nor has it ever been, to earn it, sustain it, work for it or try not to get disqualified from it. It is a home in the very heart of God that was given to you, in full, for you to enjoy and expand into.

We have to get this foundational point clear in our heads. To take steps of intimacy with God, steps of sonship and embracing our identity, we have to be secure with this one. Doubting this one is like living life on a snakes and ladders

---

[11] Galatians 3.

board; every roll you take, every movement you make has the potential to land you on a snake of doubt and derail every good bit of progress you've made.

We don't live where we used to… and we *do* live in the Father's house.

That truth has to change how we approach the rest of today. I don't want to confuse you by saying we live in the house but are also walking towards it – that is what the now and not-yet kingdom is about, and we'll dig into that more as we go along.

For this moment, however, let this one land. Living out our days from the starting point of the 'The Father's House', where we have intimate access to God Himself and all His storehouses of resources, of healing and of innovative creativity, will radically alter how we do life today.

Not in a few months' time, or in the next season. Today. You and I live from the Father's house today; we are not orphans stopping by for a quick visit, knowing that we will be asked to leave at some point. We are children of the house, who belong there.

No middle ground

The prophet Isaiah. A criminal on a cross. Peter.

Three people who had no relationship with each other. They never met or had any interactions. Yet each of them was a partaker of the same beautiful miracle.

They all experienced the radical lack of God's middle ground.

What do I mean by this?

These three men – a prophet, a criminal and a fisherman – all experienced the searing pain of conviction of sin and falling short of the mark. They also all experienced the kind of transformation from brokenness to wholeness we have been talking about.

So first, we have Isaiah, who recorded a vision and encounter he had with God in chapter 6 of his book. The prophet saw the holiness of God like no one had ever seen and it blew his mind. He saw the God of heaven in all His purity and glory and he just crumbled before Him. Isaiah knew how full of sin and brokenness he was and the world he lived in. Before the purity of God, he knew full well how in need of redeeming he was.

Second, the criminal. When Jesus was crucified, Luke's Gospel tells us, either side of Him there were two criminals also being crucified. We don't know much about them, other than whatever crime they had committed, the Romans and the authorities had decided it was worthy of crucifixion. One of the criminals in Luke 23 turned to see Jesus Christ hanging next to him, and in that moment he stepped into a revelation. He knew this man had done nothing wrong. He knew that whereas he hung there for his own sin and disregard for the law, this man Jesus was hanging there not for His own failings but for others'.

Then, lastly, we have Peter, one of Jesus' closest companions, a future leader and apostle in Jesus' church. Yet by the time we get to chapter 21 of John's Gospel we have a Peter who only a few days earlier had denied even knowing his Lord and Saviour. Circumstances had arisen that led him to completely bottle it, cave and deny he ever knew Jesus.

Peter knew about the pain of sin. He knew about the pain of not measuring up. He knew what it was like to promise Jesus everything and then fail to come through. He would have heard Jesus tell another parable about two different sons (Matthew 21:28-31) where one promised to do something for their father and then bailed out, leaving it undone. He would have been putting all these pieces together in his head.

Walking along the beach with the risen Christ as recorded in John 21, hearing Jesus ask if he loved Him, Peter knew how far he'd fallen.

Each of these three men knew the conviction of his failings. Each knew how he didn't meet the mark, and yet each one of them found a kind of restoration that still thousands of years later confounds us and perhaps even offends us. Even us in the Church. Maybe especially us in the Church.

Let's close with unpacking what happened to each of them:

Isaiah

Then one of the seraphim flew to me, having in his hand a burning coal that he had taken with tongs from the altar. And he touched my mouth and said: 'Behold, this has touched your lips; your guilt is taken away, and your sin atoned for.'

And I heard the voice of the Lord saying, 'Whom shall I send, and who will go for us?' Then I said, 'Here am I! Send me.' And he said, 'Go, and say to this people …'

(Isaiah 6:6-9)

The criminal

'We are receiving the due reward of our deeds; but this man has done nothing wrong.' And he said, 'Jesus, remember me when you come into your kingdom.' And he said to him, 'Truly, I say to you, today you will be with me in Paradise.'

(Luke 23:41-43)

Peter

'Do you love me?' … 'Lord, you know everything; you know that I love you.' Jesus said to him, 'Feed my sheep.'

(John 21:17)

Each one of these men professes his faith in God, in the midst of great heartbreak, turmoil and conviction. Each one trusts that God is good as those words come out of his mouth. Each one was lost and is asking to be found again. Each one is forgiven and restored.

And then, each one immediately gets launched into the fullness of calling.

Do you see it?

Isaiah goes from sinful and covered in shame to the chosen volunteer for God's next task.

The criminal goes from being crucified to being invited to immediately step into Paradise with Jesus, that very day.

Peter goes from the betrayer of the Lord to the Lord's chosen shepherd and guardian of His newly birthed Church.

In each case, the first thing out of God's mouth after cleansing is an invitation. An assignment. A calling. A desire for partnership. An affirmation of hope. An immediate response to the most painful kind of vulnerability a human can step into. God's love response is astounding. There is no delay.

No waiting time.

No purgatory.

No probation period.

No 'couple of months or years to rebuild trust'.

No middle ground.

They are forgiven and restored and then launched straight into the fullness of their new life.

There is not a single human in all of recorded history that would be so reckless with their trust as this. This is our God. He takes things that were once lost and makes them new again. And then He invites them to walk back home with Him, to where they belong. Talking to them all the while about the wonders He wants them to do with Him. Once we are restored in His sight, we *are* restored.

Yes the heart and soul need time to absorb this and grow into the truth of who we are. I cannot and will not compromise on preaching on maturity, character, discipline and patience. The fruit of the Spirit[12] takes time to ripen in our life; we cannot rush it and we need to trust the pace at which God chooses to lead us.

But when it comes to the completeness of the transformation, the rebirthing, the healing? For Him it is a done deal.

---

[12] Galatians 5:22-23.

4
Inside You

'So what stopped you?'

The question knocked you off whatever garden path your mind was wandering on and brought you back to the actual path you were on.

You were on the walk home, the day when the return journey started, taking those first few steps along the path, maybe only a few hundred yards from the grace collision point. That's when He asked the question you didn't realise had been churning around inside you since the moment you saw Him come running.

You tried to deflect it at first, not for any particular reason other than well-honed defence techniques and a nervousness to answer direct questions unless you know where a conversation is going.

'What do You mean, what stopped me? I mean, nothing stopped me, it was just, you know...'

That was a great answer. God would be satisfied with that.

He didn't break stride, nor break His smile.

'What stopped you from coming to Me sooner?'

Yep, it's the question you didn't want to be asked. The only answer you had was one you didn't want to hear yourself say.

Pride.

Control.

Fear.

Shame.

Twice you opened your mouth to answer and twice you came up with nothing. You didn't even realise the two of you had stopped walking and were now facing each other, tears already welling up heavy in your eyes... you were feeling it... all of it... and if you had been given a pen and paper to write down what was happening inside you, you wouldn't even have been able to form the first sentence. You just knew it was all rising up in you.

He spoke again.

'You turned around and you looked towards My house, you looked in the direction of it as best you knew, you remembered Me and you started walking. Child, I saw that. That touched My heart. Do you believe that?'

His hands were on your shoulders, His eyes locked with yours.

'I know why you couldn't come sooner, it's OK... but I need you to know why you didn't. It's going to be important in your journey, for you and for others. Come on, we can talk as we walk.'

He reached towards you and gently slipped off the strap of your backpack that had been digging into your shoulder.

'Let Me take this from here on.'

I think I was just very fortunate that my first real experience of local church was so positive. I met real people who were just trying to authentically draw nearer to God and be a family at the same time. That authenticity and community birthed in me a love for the local church and then the wider global Church. It is so unlike any other organisation on earth, and when it's working and when it's loving, it can be heaven on earth.

I love the gathering together, all the worship and the singing and hearing a preacher pull something out of the Bible that I've never seen before. I love the mission and the vision and seeing the small and big transformations that can happen in a person's life or in the local community. I love sitting in a living room with a cup of tea in my small group as someone leads us on an acoustic guitar and the Holy Spirit lands in the room. I love sitting across the table from someone and hearing their story, or celebrating their miracle with them, or even when it's painful, weeping with them in their loss. There are moments I have felt God's tangible presence when I've been on my face on the floor, or simply standing at the back watching it all unfold, that I could live in forever. The realness, the authenticity and the power of the Church when it is being what Jesus asked it to be quite simply blows me away.

It is so painful to hear people's stories when this is not the kind of church they have experienced. When their church was lukewarm or shallow, or when it was controlling or manipulative. One note of sadness I've experienced many times is when it feels like a church has little or no vision. I believe Jesus' plan for the world involves communities that are real and authentic, full of faith and transformative. Ordinary people who are encountering the real thing, for themselves, and then taking that out to the world.

Now, going for 'real' doesn't mean that I need every meeting and every sermon to be about me and my issues. Real means genuine. Authentic people, gathered in and among the presence of the real God.

This kind of living means that before people and before God *what is going on inside me* doesn't get pushed to the side, it gets brought front and centre. God desires to speak to what is going on inside you and me. Look at the first few encounters God and humanity have in Genesis. He involves Himself in the lives of Adam and Eve, of Noah and Abraham and Jacob, and in helping them He somehow manages to make it all work out for His glory. Just like with them, God wants to speak to our emotions and questions, our anxieties and our pages upon pages of prayer requests. The deep things He has placed there that have not yet awoken are on His list too. He wants to hear and speak to that internal conversation we all have inside us.

You and I were born and made to be very complex. We were made to experience this world through our emotions and feelings, as well as through our spirits and souls. Our God-designed antennae pick up the spiritual and the natural world and everything in between and all of that adds to that internal processing within us. That conversation has to be responded to. It may feel like a swirl of confusing and conflicting emotions, but it has to be addressed and responded to.

If the world and its wisdom is the only thing responding to that voice, then whatever the definition of truth or a 'good life' is for that time and era will be given in response. If it's friends and peers who mean well but don't have real wisdom, we will open ourselves up to being led in all kinds of obscure directions. If the enemy, Satan, gets his words inside us, then he will twist and coil around our heart like a snake until there is no more life or hope left in us.

There is only one voice that can speak into the inside of us and give us what we need to get to Him. There's only one voice that can reach you wherever you are, and get through whatever is going on around you.

Only one voice can adequately respond to the cry inside us.

Only one voice can bring the peace we need.

Only one voice can impart hope.

Only one voice can draw out the deep things put inside you before you were born.

Only one voice has the truth needed to anchor a life.

Only one voice can speak to our hearts in the way they need.

Only one voice can call your name and mine and bring beauty where there were 'ashes' and 'gladness' where there was 'mourning', as Isaiah 61:3 reveals.

When God speaks to you and me, the swirl of what is going on inside becomes a bridge to His transformation in us, not a barrier to it.

180

About ten years ago I experienced one of these moments. Something that was causing a lot of pain and anxiety in my heart became a bridge to God's transformation in me.

This scripture we're camped in, Luke 15, the prodigal son parable, was the setting for one of my biggest 'inside me' breakthroughs with God. For years the parable had held the place of my most beloved and treasured scripture and yet also the one piece of the Bible I was most scared of. I loved the scripture so much and found so much genuine hope in it. But I also couldn't get away from an unanswered question about it; this question led me to store up fears that I would be condemned and rejected by God because of my past choices and my struggles to live free from sin.

Essentially, because I had a lack of experience and understanding about who God was and the intimate relationship He wanted to have with me, I was terrified of Him. As I spoke about in the second chapter, I had filters over my eyes. I didn't know it at the time, but I both loved God and lived with deep fear about who He was and what He might do to me.

When I looked at the prodigal son story, I could get that the father forgave the son. I could accept that he restored him and lavished his love upon his boy. I could see that this was God. I could see it was the Father. I could see that Jesus was telling this story to give me hope and assurance of the love of God. The problem I felt inside me with the story was that I could never fully reconcile my behavioural tendencies with the forgiving capacity of God. I couldn't see past that day of celebration; the 'what next' of it all was in my head, but not in a good way.

'What if a couple of days later the son sinned again... he stole... he looked at pornography... he abused his inheritance again... would the Father forgive again, after all that forgiveness and restoration?'

For some reason, I just couldn't settle in my heart that God would forgive again. I couldn't get my head round the idea that after everything He'd already done, He'd still run out again, search for His son, and restore Him a second or a third time.

I, like everyone, have had a range of experiences of male authority figures in my life – in my family, my school teachers, with church leaders, managers and bosses. I was used to some version of the 'three strikes and you're out' mindset. It's in our culture and some version of it gets passed down through the generations. We pass on discipline techniques and values, father to son, teacher to student and so on. I knew well from my youth that if I kept pushing it (and I often did) I would get punished. I might get a couple of stays of mercy but if I kept repeating disobedience, I would get punished. I knew this mindset well; I used it as a teacher every day of my career.

As I wrestled with these thoughts I started to create a faulty mindset, a trap I couldn't get out of. I knew that in the world, if you prove yourself untrustworthy, you don't get trusted with full restoration. I felt the son in the parable had some understanding of this concept; why else would he prepare a proposal to be reduced to a slave upon his return? My experience of authority figures was that you only had so many chances to get it right, *so why would God be any different?*

There is no shortage of scriptures in the Old Testament where God punished people for seemingly small misdemeanours as well as the big ones. When I looked at these, they just fed my fear. I didn't have an appreciation for God's holiness, that before the cross, a price needed to be paid for sin, and so I couldn't understand the nature of God in those stories. He just seemed dangerous and my reasons to fear Him felt valid. As I got into the New Testament I found myself steering clear of certain books, like the book of James, also chunks of the Gospels, as the behaviour they asked for seemed unattainable for me and just left me feeling wretched.

Between 2009 and 2010 I transitioned into Catch The Fire church in London, a new non-denominational church that was born from an outpouring of the Holy Spirit that had happened in Toronto, Canada, in the 1990s, which came to be known as the Toronto Blessing. People from all over the world flocked to a little church in Toronto, not far from the airport, where God was doing miraculous things. People were encountering Him powerfully, healings were happening and lives were being restored. Some saw the movement as controversial; others saw it as water in the desert. For much of my life prior to this moment, I just saw it as something that happened somewhere else in the world, probably a bit weird, but mainly irrelevant to me. Well, this new movement started to spread around the world and one of those expressions was the recently planted church in London I was now joining. Hunger and desperation for the real God and real faith led me there. It's amazing what you'll do when you're desperate.

My first six months were a blur of the best possible kind. I heard about and experienced the Father heart of God and started to feel what it was like to have parts of my heart healed. Each Sunday was like a dousing under a waterfall of God's presence. Sometimes it was a gentle trickle and other times it was like being asked to stand still under Niagara Falls as it thundered down over me.

One particular Sunday one of the leaders, Abi Allsop, was preaching from Romans 8. She said something, mid-preach, that simply changed my entire life and the way I had been thinking. In one moment of one preach, all my years of wrestling with God, who He was and how He saw me, were suddenly directly addressed. Roughly paraphrased, this is what she said:

> There is a difference between condemnation and conviction. Condemnation ties the sin to who you are. You stole that thing, so you're a thief. You got angry about that situation, so you are an angry person. You failed at your dream, so you are a failure. You had a perverse thought, so you are a perverted person.
>
> Conviction is different; conviction looks at those same things and says, 'You're better than that, you're so much more than that sin. When you did that, you were acting below who you are. You were made for more than that. God wants to lift you up out of this

and restore you back to who you are.' That's the heart of the Father towards you.[13]

Those words changed my life.

This was a 180-degree turnaround for me.

I realised that orphans still fear condemnation.

Condemnation kicks you when you're down, holds its knee on your back and doesn't let you go.

Sons and daughters, who know who they are in Him, know that condemnation will never come from God. God will convict us for sure, but it's good. It's full of life and hope and healing. God's conviction reminds you of who you really are and helps you get back there. I realised that what had been churning inside me was a complete misunderstanding of who God was, and because I didn't know who He was, I couldn't know who I was, either. For He is the only one who can tell us who we are.

I didn't know that sons and daughters get conviction, but not condemnation. That changed everything for me. I could approach Him. It was OK. He wanted me to come near, even if my second, third or fiftieth attempt at defeating sin and selfishness had failed. He wanted to tell me who I was, and that started with trusting who He was.

The Father's house, residing there, living as a real Christian, saved and won by Jesus, is a life where there is no longer any fear about the condemnation of God coming against you (Romans 8:1). Condemnation has been removed from your life and it is unredeemed thinking to believe that your sin can override the power of the blood of Christ.

You and I are free.

The darkest parts of you, the heaviest moments of shame and the most deeply hidden fears can be known by God, and you will be adored and loved as you trust God with those things. His presence is a safe place for us to be real and honest.

---

[13] Abi Allsop. Used with permission.

Yes, our heavenly Dad will discipline and correct us when we need it. I'm not throwing discipline out – Scripture is really clear on the fact that discipline can be good for us and needed.[14] Yes, God will convict me of my sin. Yes, He will discipline me, like a good Father disciplines his child. But no, He won't ever condemn me. It is spiritually impossible for a believer covered in the blood of Jesus, the Lamb of God, to experience condemnation from God.

God is my safe place and yours. Learning this and believing it didn't cause me to stop fearing the Lord in the biblical sense, nor did it decrease my belief in His holiness or purity. It just caused me to not be afraid of being His child. Sons and daughters of God know His power, but they also know His untamable love.

Turning and running

If you've been a Christian more than five minutes, you'll know you can't do this life based on effort. You can certainly spend a few decades or more trying to prove you're the exception to that rule, but ultimately you'll end up at the same conclusion.

Paul called out the Galatians on this. He was pretty hard in chapter 3 of his letter to them. They had been saved by grace like the rest of us, but were now trying to base that salvation on the works they did and the fruit they bore. In our day, there are entire world religions that have this as their core belief and essentially their way to heaven. They teach that hard work, good deeds or storing up karma will be the key to salvation. Not so for Christians. It was grace that saved us and grace that will continue to save us.[15]

Works and effort are the fruit of a saved life, but not the seal of it.

---

[14] Psalm 94:12; Proverbs 3:11-12; Hebrews 12:9-11.
[15] Ephesians 2:8-9.

To walk the journey with God, to be people who say, 'My Father's house is my home,' and mean it, to be sons and daughters and not orphans, requires both a revelation about who God is and an internal shift inside us.

The parable of the prodigal son offers two phrases that give us a way into the road we want to walk when the issue of works and grace comes to the fore.

> when he came to himself (v17)

> But while he was still a long way off, his father saw him and felt compassion (v20)

Two statements. One about a son finally remembering who he always was. One about the father being who he's always been. The beauty of these two truths and how they are used by Jesus is how they invert so many of our expectations about God when He encounters our mess.

We turn and He runs towards us.

We stumble and He embraces us.

We expect punishment and He pulls us into a chest wrought by compassion.

We profess that we're not trustworthy any more and He places a ring of authority on our finger.

We offer slavery and He re-establishes sonship.

We remind Him of our failure and He reminds us of His covenant.

Because of the cross of Messiah Jesus, this is how it now works.

This is the way it is supposed to work.

Regardless of whether you have been a believer since birth, been pursuing God for decades or really don't know where you stand with it all, this God of seemingly counter-intuitive acts of redemption and love is the only God there has ever been. He's been this loving forever. He's been this kind always. He's been offering this relationship... since day one.

The more I have orbited this parable, the more I have come to realise that 'coming to yourself' is such a key part of God's process. The younger son stood back, just for a moment, long enough to look at his life and realise how far he was from what he used to live in.

I've tried to force this step. Oh, man, I have tried to 'come to myself', flick a switch, say in a few quick moments how sorry I am and how much I've lost the plot and do the fast track repentance thing to just get my winning streak back.

God 'looks on the heart' (1 Samuel 16:7). He called a forgotten shepherd boy from the pastures and in front of his older, seemingly more impressive brothers, had him anointed as the king of a nation, because of his heart.

I cannot move any further down the road of sonship without coming to my senses and realising how much I truly need God. My heart, as it really is, has to be opened up to Him. There's no specifically worded prayer, no sacrificial act and no good deed that will balance out the sin. It is a heart yielded, perhaps re-yielded, to Jesus that will get us off our knees and onto the road. That's what the son was doing. He wasn't playing a game. He really meant it.

There is no other way.

I have in my mind a picture of a compass spinning in random directions, completely confused, unable to find any bearing. The moment of 'coming to ourselves' is like the introduction of magnetic north to that compass. Suddenly it has a direction. This is what that step does for us.

Our lives, what you and I have before us, are meant to go from days stumbling on a dirt path to an eternal home in the Father's house characterised by freedom and celebration. No human being starts in the house of God redeemed and ready for glory. We've all fallen short. We all need a Saviour. We all need to get it clear in our heads that acting good sometimes or 'for the most part' isn't going to cut it when we stand before the most pure being in the universe. We all need to come to ourselves and realise that we need Him.

The beauty of doing this is that the moment we do, even while we are 'still a long way off', He sees us with nothing but compassion and this drives Him to run like the wind towards us. Such is His desire to redeem us. Our little moment of turning towards Him is met by His life-changing moment of running towards us and scooping us up.

If your life has been characterised by effort or fixing, by trying to get through the narrow gate [16] by your careful adjustments or good behaviour, then I would encourage you to consider this alternative. We turn, we get real, we face Him, and He comes running. Is this what you want? Or do you prefer the other thing? You and I always have a choice.

It's important to note that at this point we could be in danger of thinking our moment of self-realisation and turning causes God to do the forgiving… perhaps we could start thinking that it is us who begin the process of our own restoration? By dissecting this parable, are we saying that somehow God only starts putting on His shoes when He sees us coming over the horizon?

The reassuring reality is that you and I will find in our turning that He was behind us, whispering close all the time, always desiring our return. He had, in fact, decided long before we came along that He was going to come running for us. That's where we're going next.

Plan A

The cross wasn't a reaction.

I react to things.

When I'm thinking clearly, when I'm at peace, I *respond*.

When I'm wrought up or wound up, I *react*.

I think there is a difference between the two.

My reactions come from the *as yet to be healed* parts of me. The raw, untamed parts of me I haven't let Jesus handle or get

---

[16] Matthew 7:13-14.

to yet. They betray where I am still insecure or still trying to hold on to control. My reactions are not enjoyed by those around me all that much, if I'm being honest.

I love eating food when it is hot. I enter major distress when the food comes out of the oven and is not immediately plated up and enjoyed. My wife knows this, but sometimes she likes to get a few extra things out of the cupboard for her dinner, some salad dressing, a different drink and so on. In the early months of our marriage, as we had dinner, I would be ready, sitting with my plate before me, and Abbi would be moving around getting her things ready. She didn't have the same concern about the food temperature. As I sat there watching my plate slowly cooling down and all that lovely sizzling dying out, I would start to feel distressed. As I hadn't let Jesus into that area of my life, my poor wife got my grumpy, passive-aggressive reactions rather than grace-filled and patient responses. I would tell her what I thought she should do to speed it up and make plans to stop it from happening again in the future. She didn't get peace or understanding from me, she just got the ugly parts of a husband who really could just use a microwave if it were that big a deal. Not cool, Alistair.

Reactions are rarely what we want them to be. Responses are different, though. Usually they have some level of filtering. When I respond, I pray before I speak. I ask for wisdom before I move. I try to make sure the renewed mind is calling the shots, not the orphaned mind. When I think ahead, I prepare myself for what is coming, and as a result my responses tend to hurt people less. The side benefit of this is that my responses make me look better than my reactions do.

For the longest time I thought the cross was *a reaction* of God towards us all.

Jesus dying on the cross was in my mind a last-ditch attempt to get things right after all our failures at trying to be pure. I imagined God saying in heaven, 'Well, if you want something doing you'd better do it yourself!' Somewhere in my theology I saw God as frustrated, annoyed with us all, throwing the dice one last time and inviting His dutiful but probably reluctant Son into the whole endeavour. I didn't think of Jesus Christ as Messiah Yeshua, the prophesied one. I saw Him as a problem-solver for a people who were on their last chance.

I was *so* wrong.

Whether you understand the nuances of the pre-Christ foreshadowings in the Old Testament law or not, the fact is that the cross is the culmination of a plan that was set in motion a long time ago. It was decided before creation began, before a single human being was brought into existence. Long before any of us were born, it was agreed in heaven that God was going to come to earth as one of us and die as one of us, and for us.

The cross of Christ was God's predetermined response to what was about to come. It wasn't His emotional reaction to the situation going south. It was a response to what was coming, not a reaction to what had already happened.

The cross was God's plan A.

Before Adam and Eve started plucking fruit from trees in the garden, God the Father, Son and Holy Spirit decided that to make us meant to save us. To make the world would mean to one day rescue the world. Every child born of a woman was going to be born into a sinful world because we were not going to ever be mature enough to live a free life of purity on our own. We were all going to mess it up. We were all going to need a Saviour to come and die for us. We were all going to need grace to come down from heaven and turn our hearts around.

Years of sacrifices, animal blood, tablets of stone and priestly functions were all really setting the scene for the fact that by ourselves this thing wasn't going to work. Sin needed dealing with. A sacrifice that would last was needed.

The only way we could get free from our brokenness, the only way we could step into the heaven-on-earth way of living, was if God Himself intervened and balanced out both sides of the equation. That's what Jesus did when He hung on the cross at Calvary and when He rose from the dead three days later. He took our place. He removed us from the pivotal part of the

75

equation. Only God could take the burden of all humankind on His shoulders and only a human being could do it on behalf of humanity. Jesus, God in human form, stood in the gap. The book of Revelation says He is the Lamb crucified 'from the creation of the world'.[17] That means that God's choice to die on that tree was made long before Adam and Eve ever made their choice to sin.

God is the One who stirs us to 'come to ourselves' and realise by how far we've missed the mark. Together as one, Father, Spirit and Son, God comes running for us while we are 'a long way off'. Jesus wraps around us and clothes us. The Holy Spirit fills us with hope again. The Father restores our identity.

This is the only way it was ever going to work.

God doing His part and our part. And us simply needing to say 'yes' to the plan and the outcome.

Jesus told the story of that son meeting his father on the path of his life knowing that the cross was coming for Him. The cross was going to make it possible. The cross was going to balance the scales for each one of us. Jesus knew as He told this story about a restored ring of authority and a cloak covering the stain, that it would be His death and resurrection that would make it all possible.

It was all beautiful grace.

The cross is the centrepiece of all creation. It's the reason any of us can raise our heads to heaven and say, *'Abba...Daddy.'*[18] It's the reason we don't get obliterated when the Father hugs us on that path. Love, justice and mercy were released at the cross. This should speak answers to the things going on inside us, that we were valuable enough for Jesus to go through all that; His care for us knew no limits.

The cross was always going to be the way we got free. That should be a reassuring thought.

---

[17] Revelation 13:8, NIV.
[18] See Romans 8:15.

5
The Trouble with Truth

That spot in the dirt path where the grace collision happened has become something of a place of pilgrimage in your life. You think about it often, reminding yourself how much love was launched at you, how much freedom was uncapped in you. It gives you strength, and that's a good and needed thing some days.

There are times when you find yourself wandering down that steady firm road to where it joins the dirt path where it all happened. Sometimes you go and sit on the grass and stare at the spot. On other occasions you just stand there for a moment before moving on. It's a complex thing going on inside you, as there is thankfulness for the breakthrough rising up, but also questions about what your life is meant to look like now.

You don't hang around too long at the spot on the path. You know well enough to head home.

That's where you belong.

One evening in the house, you find yourself doing things somewhat absent-mindedly. You lay the table in silence, and pick and poke your food on the plate all throughout dinner. You seem distant and you're not quite sure why.

The Father looks at you and you struggle to hold His gaze very long.

'What is wrong with me today?' you ask yourself internally.

Excusing yourself, you make your way upstairs.

Along the corridor and into your room. Closing the door, turning the key in the lock for some reason, then switching the table light on, you find yourself standing in front of the mirror. Looking at the reflection, you stare at yourself silently.

Just you alone in the room.

Gradually, that thing you didn't want to admit starts bubbling up inside you.

You don't feel like you think you should feel.

You got restored and redeemed... you encountered the Father's love... you've seen miracles... prophetic words have been spoken over you... you encountered the love of the Trinity for you and it was good and beautiful.

But this soul journey is taking longer than you wanted it to, there's still so much of the old you seemingly operating as if it was alive and well and unaffected by your restoration. Your mind still churns up unhelpful thoughts. Painful thoughts that you don't want anyone to know about. You're so aware of how selfish you can be. How deliberately sinful and independent you still can be. You know you still watch other people in the house, you see how they interact with the Father and with each other and it makes you feel... less. Even though you know you shouldn't.

You know that you're in the right place and that the truth about who you are is the truth... but you can't help but think that it should be easier than it is. Why are you not living as a child of God in the way you know you could? Why does it feel like your body is doing a 50/50 share between the old you and the new you?

You stare at the mirror and open your mouth and start speaking out into the empty room: Jesus, the truth is meant to set me free; sometimes I feel it and then sometimes I don't. There are moments I feel like I am exactly who You say I am, and then other times I just feel like 100 per cent the old me. Why does it feel like I'm... not free yet?'

'Oh "the truth will set you free",[19] He replies and pauses. 'When you trust it.'

We are going to look deeper at the transformation we all want. The transformation that is given as a grace gift to every adopted

---

[19] John 8:32.

son and daughter of God. It's a Holy Spirit job; it's not an effort or a discipline thing, even though it will require us to roll our sleeves up and get rid of some old habits and make some new, better ones. Transformation only comes by the intervention of the Holy Spirit, the 'Spirit of truth',[20] as He personally lands right down in the areas of us that are broken, insecure and ugly.

The kind of transformation process we want can be looked at from a bird's-eye view as well as through a microscope. In the next chapter we're going to look under the microscope at what may be a deeply personal issue for you. I would refer to it here as that lone thing, that sin, that pain, that stronghold that has stood above all others in your head and heart that feels like it refuses to change. It will be different for all of us, but every one of us will face one sin, temptation or limitation that can only be conquered through a radical level of trust in God's power.

We can't successfully approach this territory in general and personal terms without passing through the gate of one particular topic, however.

Truth.

What is true and what isn't is the foundation for what is considered wisdom. The kingdom is built on truth. And everything that is not the kingdom is built on the other thing. We have to walk over this truth ground on the road to the Father's house for all the other future steps to be taken safely.

Calling, gifting, dreaming, operating in signs and wonders, doing supernatural miracles and being a nation-changer; those are all things in the Father's heart for His sons and daughters to do. However, without these steps behind the scenes of transformation, without seeing the value of truth in our little lives, we could step into our callings as unsafe, unhealed and dangerously broken influencers. God wants so much more for us than that.

The trouble with truth is, it has to be fuelled by trust.

---

[20] See John 14:17; 15:26; 16:13.

Truth will not 'set you free'[21] if you don't trust it.

Reformation in your life won't come if the truth isn't trusted.

Foundations have to be placed in the solid, trusted ground of truth for the building to go high.[22]

You'll never overcome the lie if you don't trust that the truth is better.

Trust is huge when it comes to talking about the truth.

Some may look at the truth from a distance and compliment it, like it is some vintage car, but a car with no fuel in it isn't going to take you anywhere. If we want to go somewhere with our lives, this is the planetary object we have to orbit round. The subject is crucial and its consequences will make the difference between you and me experiencing freedom, breakthrough and maturity in our lives, and not.

I must have heard thousands of sermons, so many scriptures, so many truths being spoken and had so many seeds scattered in the soil of my life. And so much of it I have forgotten.

Is that your experience? I feel embarrassed almost to admit that I've probably forgotten 90 per cent of what has been preached at me in the last fifteen to twenty years. Does that mean it was a waste of time sitting there and listening to those words and truths? No, of course not. Like a good healthy meal, the nutrients of the words were absorbed and put to good use inside me; nothing was wasted. I just didn't have the capacity to remember everything verbatim, even if I wished I could.

Fortunately, that isn't the only way we absorb truth.

Whether our lives are on the ascendancy, or just struggling to get out of the pit, many of us have heard words of truth spoken to us, over us or around us.

> For God so loved the world, that he gave his only Son.
> (John 3:16)

---

[21] John 8:32.
[22] Matthew 7:24-27.

For freedom Christ has set us free.
(Galatians 5:1)

God … will not let you be tempted beyond your ability.
(1 Corinthians 10:13)

Ask … seek … knock, and it will be opened to you
(Matthew 7:7)

For nothing will be impossible with God
(Luke 1:37)

So many truths that have lasted the test of time. Truths that have not been stamped out over the centuries or disproved by philosophy, or science, or atheist dictators. We have heard these truths spoken over us by pastors and preachers, by friends, by God Himself leaping off the pages of our Bibles or echoing through our hearts. I'm guessing that if you're a Christian, you have had the promises of God shared with you so many times you could not count them. If you're not, in today's culture in the West, at least, everyone has access to the all-time bestselling book (the Bible). We don't have a shortage of truth in our lives.

However, what we do time and time again is hear it, say it or read it *and assume* it has become embedded deep within us. Absorbed. Assimilated. Fused with us. Right?

'I heard that sermon, read that book, went to that conference, saw that preacher's meme, so I must be living in it now, right?'

Sometimes this is the case. Sometimes the Word of God speaks so loudly and so clearly it changes everything. When my friend Abi Allsop preached about the difference between condemnation and conviction, it was honestly a life-changing moment for me. That was truth that could have taken decades worth of slowly trusting and believing in to see established, but was deeply planted in me *in an instant.* Moments like this are powerful and significant and should lead us to worship and adoration. But God does not operate solely in moments such as this, and to believe that He does would be to deny some extremely biblical ways He interacts with and develops His children.

In the vast majority of cases, He takes His time. He works in us over the course of our lives. The truth entering us and changing us often takes decades. The danger we in the Western Church all too regularly flirt with is that we hear something good, something true, and assume it has automatically taken root in us.

Often a great preach or sermon we heard was great because the anointing of God was on it. Equally we could be benefiting from the years of godly formation in the person's own life, their pursuit of God, their decades of disciplined growth and hunger for God. It could be hours of prayer and study and seeking the Lord that were put into it. The list goes on. It's crazy to think that after just forty minutes of sitting there and listening to a word, we can walk away thinking that 'we've got it all now… thanks… all good from here'.

Being immersed in the truth of God, the Word of life, is not something we can achieve over a weekend. Many of us have dangled our feet in the Word, in the truth. Splashed around a bit. What we are talking about here is the difference between dipping into truth and being submerged in it. I'll explain it in the way my pastor, Stu Glassborow,[23] taught me, by looking at the difference between a pickle and a cucumber, and what that can tell us about the difference between a life dipped in truth and one immersed in it.

Bapto/baptizo

I don't like gherkins in my burgers; honestly, what are they doing in there? A bit of lettuce and some onion is fine, a little bit of crunch is good, but a pickle or gherkin is just too much

---

[23] Stuart Glassborow, senior leader, Catch The Fire London. Used with permission.

for me. I have something of a reflex muscle that leads me to automatically search for any rogue gherkins before I bite into a burger.

Now, regardless of my opinion on it, let's hover over that vegetable for a moment, as it has something to do with the Greek words the Bible uses for 'baptism' in the New Testament.

The word *bapto* is used a number of times in the New Testament. In Luke 16:19-31, Jesus tells a story of a rich man and a poor man called Lazarus. We have a painful moment in the story where the rich man, now dwelling in the fires of Hades, begs Abraham (who is in heaven) to send the former poor beggar Lazarus, whom he always ignored and failed to help in life, and have him dip his finger into water and cool his tongue.

Bapto is used here and it means 'to dip'.

In John 13, Jesus is having His last meal with the disciples before He goes to the cross. He has just told His friends that one of them is going to betray Him and they are all asking who it is going to be. Jesus answers them and says it will be the one who will receive a morsel of bread from Jesus once He has dipped it (v26). He then proceeds to give it to Judas. The word used here is the same word as in Luke 16:24. Again, *bapto* here means 'to dip'.

In Revelation 19, John's vision of heaven turns to Jesus. John speaks of Jesus being 'clothed in a robe dipped in blood, and the name by which he is called is The Word of God' (v13). *Bapto* once again is used here, and it means 'to dip'.

We can see that this word's meaning is pretty clear. You put something in, you pull it out again. That is what dipping is.

Bapto is not the only word for baptism that we find in the New Testament, however. The other word is very similar, but the nuance of it has the potential to radically alter how we see the transformation God has done in our lives, and how it might affect our experience of being His sons and daughters. The word we are thinking of is *baptizo*. It means being dipped repeatedly and continually. It is used a number of times in the New Testament. In Acts it describes the men and women baptised in the name of Jesus Christ. Paul uses it repeatedly in his letters to the Romans, Corinthians and Galatians to talk about our new transformed nature in Christ.

Galatians 3:27 says we have been 'baptized into Christ' and 'have put on Christ', becoming completely His.

Baptizo means *fully immersed.*

Immersion

There was a Greek poet called Nicander who was alive around the year 200 BC. Somehow, a recipe he wrote for making pickles survived the passage of time. In his recipe he uses both the words *bapto* and *baptizo* in a way that creates a useful analogy for what we're talking about. The instruction is to take a cucumber, dip it (*bapto*) into boiling water and then baptise it (*baptizo*) in vinegar. Then after it has been left immersed in vinegar for a few days, you have your pickle. [24] When opened up to its spiritual implications, we've really got something.

The first is a dipping in and out of water. The second is an immersion in the vinegar.

Other descriptions have been used over the years. So if pickling and making gherkins doesn't work for you as an image, picture meat marinating overnight, or a T-shirt tie dyed, changing in nature. It's the immersion that causes a change of state. It alters what the thing was before it was immersed. It makes it something new. The cucumber becomes a pickle. It's different. Its nature has been changed. It's not what it was before.

OK. Let's do application, even though I'm guessing you're already there. Being dipped in God's presence, in God's truth, isn't enough. It's beautiful and powerful and it is life-changing. But single dippings and momentary meetings with Him are not

---

[24] www.biblestudytools.com/lexicons/greek/nas/baptizo.html (accessed 20th October 2019).

enough to cause the person-wide transformation He wants me and you to experience.

What you and I need has to be a *baptizo* experience. It has to be being immersed daily, continually and repeatedly in Him. In His truth. In the Word. In Jesus. In the Holy Spirit. In the Father.

Immersed… marinated… dyed… pickled in Him.

I realised, when I first started taking those first steps back home on the road to the Father's house, that the transformation I was seeking in my life was not coming when I only dipped my foot in the truth. However, in the areas where I let it overflow and immerse me, I was seeing change.

When I have that real encounter with Him on that path I get the opportunity to have Christ in me, as Colossians 1:27 says. My identity gets fused with His. I become newly me, Him in me.

If I want it, that is.

I can dip my toe in and take some portion of it and keep some control. I can actually war against the transformation He's doing in me. It seems crazy, but we do it.

Or, alternatively, we can just be all in. That sounds much better, right? It is, but you have to be all in every day, day after day, and that requires commitment.

The ones who are all in, however, get the truth of the next part in Colossians 3:3: 'For you have died, and your life is hidden with Christ in God.' I'm now hidden *in* Him *with* God.

I don't even understand how that works.

Somehow He is in me… and at the same time, I'm hidden in Him… and with God?

It is a beautiful mystery we get to start taking steps in as we move on from that moment of collision. I missed it for so long. I didn't trust God's truth that I was new in Him and He in me. I was scared, I think. Maybe I also wasn't around that many people who knew that truth for themselves. Finding a community of people who truly immerse themselves in God's truth and His Word might be one of the best decisions you ever make.

Chlo Glassborow gets this. Every morning she starts her day the same way: 'Hi, Holy Spirit.'[25]

She gets that He's so close, she's in Him and He's in her. She's living an immersed life, not a life that is getting tied in knots thinking about a list of religious boxes to tick, but a life that is relationally close to God.

Why do some people seem to have better lives as Christians than others?

I'm not a betting man, but if I were I'd say it's got something to do with how immersed they are in the truth. The truth is Jesus (John 14:6) and the truth is His Word (John 17:17). And He really does transform when He is trusted.

I love having baths, always have. I know that if I dip my foot in a hot bath and pull it out after a minute I'll see a red mark on my skin from the heat; the skin will feel hot but it's really just the outside of the foot that's feeling it. If I sit in the bath for an hour, the water heats the whole of me up, inside and out, and by the time I get out of the bath, my whole body has regulated to the temperature. I have sweated sometimes for hours after having a bath because I had it so hot and was in it too long. This is what immersion in truth does; it affects all of us from the inside out.

The truth is a belt

One of my heroes is a girl I'll call Kaley.[26]

Kaley was maybe fourteen when I first met her. We met at a Christian youth event and I was only a few years older than her. She was a feisty, spirited, independent kind of girl. I'm not quite sure how she found herself at the youth event; maybe it was her family's involvement in the local church, maybe she just had that one friend who hung on and kept the God connection going

[25] Chlo Glassborow, senior leader, Catch The Fire London. Used with permission.
[26] Name changed and testimony used with permission.

through the tough times. I don't know. What I do know is that once I started to get to know her, I saw just how much more she was dealing with than the rest of us.

She had lost her mum when she was younger. This had caused all kinds of pain as she grew up. She was now feeling the pull between being the good upper-middle-class girl she had been raised to be and the popular, desirable young woman she was finding others classified her as. I was in the upper ages of the youth group and was dipping (*bapto*) my toes into pastoral ministry for the first time, so we had chats and conversations about life and God on a regular basis.

I remembered those conversations, hearing about the drinking, the partying, the men and the police and so on. It all seemed to be snowballing. Each incident seemed to be worse than the last. I remember one evening, sitting on the steps outside a meeting hall at some youth event, hearing her talk about how hard things were getting, and then she slowly lifted up her sleeves to show the cut and slice marks she had made on her arms.

This was the first time in my life I had seen anything like this. Sadly, it was not the last.

She was trying to be so many people, failing at who she was supposed to be, unsure of who she really was, and trying to get control of what she was going through. Somehow her faith was still in there somewhere, somehow she had managed to not close the door to God... but she was not free.

Out of the blue one day, a friend recommended to her a year-out discipleship programme at a church somewhere up north. The church was known to have pretty strict boundaries and values for the protection of all the young people who did a discipleship year with them. I'll be honest, when I heard of the place it sounded pretty inflexible. I didn't understand at the time that some things were worth protecting with strong boundaries. By a miracle of God that I still don't quite understand, Kaley agreed to go. She spent a year there experiencing what I think could be best described as a *slow miracle*. She was surrounded by truth day in and day out.

She got into her Bible, into worship, into fellowship. She started allowing healing to get into her heart. She allowed the bandages to be taken off and her wounds to be looked at by Jesus. She got surrounded by a community that desired her… for who she was, not for how she looked or what they could get from her, but for who God had created her to be. They helped her see that she was, in fact, a daughter of God, with a room in His house prepared just for her (John 14:2).

She started going on outreaches to local council estates, started speaking to young girls caught up in drugs and drink and affairs and self-harm. She started speaking truth to these girls and she used herself as the prime example of how far this Jesus would go to redeem someone.

Pretty soon she met a young man, a really good man. They fell in love, they got married and about five minutes later they got pregnant. A young family began to grow out of a place where only scars and bruises had once been. Fast forward fifteen years and this young woman has completed a theology degree, is raising two beautiful children, is a wife and is heading up a national ministry that reaches out to those who don't know God yet, and introduces them to their creator and healer, Jesus.

And she's doing it all with unmistakable joy.

This is what a life redeemed by truth can look like.

Jesus said in John 14:6 and John 8:32 that 'I am the way, and the truth, and the life' and that 'the truth will set you free'. The road to the Father's house is a road paved with bricks of truth. We have to walk on the truth to get to His home.

In the armour of God in Ephesians 6, the truth is a belt (v14). It surrounds us. It holds things together. It holds things in a good kind of tension. Kaley is one of my heroes because she decided to put on the 'belt of truth' and never take it off. She could have rejected it for being constricting. She could have cast it off and said, 'I don't need boundaries, I don't need absolutes, and I don't need to be told what to do.' She could have chosen to continue to do it her own way and kept her independence.

She didn't.

She decided to give up being a slave to sin and to exchange it for being a slave to love. She stopped serving one master to sit at the feet of another. She encountered Jesus in a fresh and new way and it changed everything. Humbling herself and allowing Him to enter her life, she was vulnerable enough to let Him transform that life. To do this meant sharing her testimony, re-entering those painful memories and choosing to let her mess be a testimony of healing.

This is hard stuff. It's the real thing. This kind of choice and transformation doesn't happen over a weekend and it doesn't happen free of opposition, either external or internal. When I am tired, when it's been a long day and I flop down on the sofa and have the worst body posture a guy could have, one of the first things that I want to do is *take off my belt*. So I slip it off and release some of the tension it brings, and then I don't feel so bad about indulging in that food or drink that is going to accompany my rest time. It's also very easy to remove the 'belt of truth' so we can relax a bit when it suits us.

It is very easy to accidentally nurture a way of living where we compromise on truth depending on how we are feeling and how tough a week we're having. We will have a lot of company in that place of thinking, but it won't be the kind of company we want. I think the younger son found that out in the 'far country'[27] he fled to, and the older son found it out among his friends out there in the fields. Neither group of people is recorded to have encouraged the sons to return home.

I tell Kaley's story all over the place, not because it has a good ending, but because it shows the evidence of what prolonged trust in Jesus births in your life. She didn't earn any of it, but she trusted in the truth of His words over her life. She immersed herself in those truths, she lived like they were real…

---

[27] Luke 15:13.

and found the very face of God looking down on her in love as she did. Kaley and her husband are an advert for the love of Jesus. They are an advert for the presence of God's truth transforming a life. The world will stop and listen to stories like Kaley's because you cannot argue with transformation.

We have to get this trust thing. We have to accept the empowering grace God offers us to give us the ability to trust Him, rather than try to be heroes and do it all ourselves in our own strength. It's that important.

Simple trust opens the door to so many life-altering moments in God.

When it's real, it is often done away from the stage and the crowds. It's usually too raw and too real to make it on to many social media posts. Almost no one other than you and God will see the moments when it happens. When we do it, though, when we trust Him and His truth, we discover who He is, who we are, what is true and what is a downright lie. Trust makes transformation possible.

The trouble with truth is that it will always need to be trusted for it to work in our lives. Understanding isn't necessarily required all the time; like the plane I fly on, I don't understand every element of the mechanics that keeps it in the air, but you can bet I've considered whether I trust it can fly before I get on board. Once I do, it takes me somewhere.

God, give me what I need from heaven to trust You, who You are and what You say. I know when I do start trusting You more with each step, I'm going to see the breakthrough I need and the grace-flooded life You promise. I know when I trust that You are everything You say You are that I'll find that I'm everything You say I am too.

> If you abide in my word, you are truly my disciples, and you will know the truth, and the truth will set you free.
> (John 8:31-32)

6
Parasite

Long-sleeved shirts.

Who would have thought something so simple would reveal such profound and painful truths.

You've been wearing long-sleeved shirts for a while now. In one sense you absolutely knew you were doing it. Every morning when you reached inside your wardrobe to pick your day's outfit, a little flicker of a memory would spark, something in the corner of your eye would flash and you would remember. And instead of reaching for a T-shirt or tank top, you instead chose something long that would reach down to your wrists.

Here's the thing. There was no hiding your brokenness when the Father met you on the path that day. You were covered in all the mess and sin, and there was no avoiding it or pretending it wasn't there. Let's be honest, if He couldn't have seen it, He would have smelt it. There was no hiding the wounds.

In a way, it felt like everything was attended to and seen to in one go. The cloak that was put on you, the real covering of Jesus Himself, stayed on you all the way back home. It never slipped off or came loose. It wrapped all around you.

However, that evening the wounds had to be dressed. You sat in a bath being washed by God Himself and there was one wound you were more aware of, more anxious about being seen than any other. You shifted your body subtly and cautiously, just doing enough to adjust yourself, to keep it out of notice, out of view.

The shame attached to this wound was etched on your face and on your heart.

This wasn't the wound of a terrible circumstance, or some level of mismanagement of your life. This was the wound caused by a parasite. This was caused by a very deliberate attack directed at you.

You had a genuine need and longing for comfort and love, but like an addiction, the way it expressed itself got twisted and ended up causing so much pain. Now this wound along your arm, the bruises and the cuts, is being looked at by God Almighty.

This is the one thing that you have tried to fix above all others, before God or people saw it.

Instead, here you are with it fully exposed to Him, unsure of whether it is the Father, Jesus or the Holy Spirit or all of them together as one… but what you do know is that in this moment, as you sit in that bath, God Himself is kneeling by your side, running that sponge along your skin, over that mark and into that wound.

The journey you have taken, walking the road to the Father's heart, trusting in the truth that you are not condemned and that you are an adopted child, that you are new, has all led to the point where you feel you can finally give this part of you over to Him too. So you turn and shift your body and let him see the cuts and scars that were done to you and that you consented and allowed to be done. He looks at you and smiles deeply and lovingly, and you know you are safe and loved and things are never going to be the same again. He's seen the worst and He smiles and loves you still.

You are so thankful for that moment, but… well, that was 'then' and you're living in 'now'.

That was 'day one' back in the house. That was just before the party and celebration and the fattened calf and the best night of your life. It's been days, months, maybe even years since that 'day one' experience and a lot of healing has come, a lot of freedom; a lot of dependency on other things has been let go of. You have been making progress and are thankful for that. However, there is still this one thing, this one wound, and it is still to fully heal. At one time it was your biggest comfort, maybe your strongest control method or source of stability when pressure and *stress arose. Whatever it was, you know the remnants of that wound are still there, and there are times when it can feel in small or in significant ways like it's not healing the way it should.*

So even though He's seen it and it still lingers, you know there are still moments when you try to keep it away from any attention. Lock it down. Use those long-sleeved shirts to keep it out of sight. Hope it will go away. Hope no one will ask you about it.

Like so many men and women, you have had the experience of receiving a wound and desperately desiring that it be healed... yet also allowing it to continue, even drawing pleasure or comfort from it.

'Child of mine...'

He steps alongside you, side by side.

'It's time. Don't be afraid, you're not on your own.'

A nail-scarred hand rests warmly on your shoulder.

We've got to go here, because this one is lethal. False comforts, addictions, unaddressed childhood pain. We have to open the lid on it.

Sin is a parasite.

A parasite is an organism that lives in or on another organism, the host. It lives and survives by taking the nutrients, essentially the life force, of the host it's attached to. The host does not benefit from this association; it's harmful to it, it's damaging.

This is what sin does. It feeds off us. It lives off us. We gain nothing. We think we get something like a temporary reward, but it is like delectable food turning to ash in our mouths. Sin taints. It doesn't satisfy. Its strength is drawn from ours.

When I was about fifteen years old I was at a youth group evening meeting. After a sweet time of worship, we gathered and talked about the armour of God from Ephesians 6. We got into groups to pray for each other after the talk, and pray that armour 'on' each other. One of my friends turned to me and said:

When I was praying for you I saw you covered in this amazing armour, but then the picture moved over to this thing on your arm; it was like a small creature, like a pet. The more I looked at it the more I realised it was not a pretty creature; it was sinister-looking. It had the façade of being a nice pet, but when I looked down at its feet I saw these talons that were digging into your arm and drawing blood.

You were wearing the armour of God all over your body, but you'd taken it off over this part of your arm so the creature could rest there. I even saw you stroking it. You didn't realise this creature you were allowing on your arm was actually evil and wanted to paralyse you. It's not your friend.

I didn't have language for the 'prophetic' at that point in my life. Words of knowledge about what I was going through or 'pictures' from God were not familiar to me yet.[28] However, what my friend had just done was give me a prophetic picture from God about what was going on in my life at that exact moment. About what I'd allowed to settle in my life. What I'd not only let into my personal space but even into my 'secret place'.

My open door

A few years before that moment in the youth group, I had been getting ready to move from primary school into secondary school. I had tests to take to get into a particularly good school and I was pretty nervous, as in that stage of my life I really didn't consider myself to be academic. I threw myself into sports and drama and creative things, but not so much the subjects they were going to be testing me on. I often got by with a mixture of what felt like good luck and pulling the rabbit out of the hat on exam day. I think it was a strategy that made both my parents

---

[28] 1 Corinthians 14:6.

and teachers nervous and put them in a semi-permanent state of anxiety about how I was doing.

Growing up, I would spend vast amounts of time in my bedroom playing games, or off on my own made-up adventures, rather than doing my work. I didn't want the label of a 'worker', far more enjoying being a 'free spirit'. Despite not being a churchgoing child, God and I used to chat all the time in my room. I'd always stop to explain my games to Him or tell Him how I was; it just came naturally to me, no one taught me to do it. As a result, my room, my alone time, always felt like something special to me. I got a lot of life from it, though it also had a level of escapism to it. I could hide from my work in an adventure.

I ended up getting a TV in my room in my early teens. It didn't seem like anything to be concerned about. It was just something that I could watch cartoons and movies on without having to fight for the remote. One night, alone in my room, long after lights out, I started flicking channels. I wasn't looking for anything in particular, I just had never surfed the TV channels this late at night before and was curious.

Suddenly, the screen landed on the image of a man and woman starting to have sex. It was clearly some racy B-movie. By modern cultural standards it was very modest, but to the thirteen-year-old me, it was like an adrenaline shot to the centre of my brain. I reacted. I responded. I remembered what the boys at school said you did when you saw stuff like that. I copied.

Maybe this little 'harmless' experience is something you can associate with. Maybe you had your own version of finding something illicit and allowing yourself to indulge in it for a moment. I suppose we all have some experience in our lives of going after what felt like a forbidden pleasure. An opportunistic moment. Some low-hanging fruit on the tree we were told to avoid.

For me it was a moment of pseudo pleasure followed immediately by a moment of tangible shame. I felt like I had done something wrong. I had crossed a line I didn't know I'd been approaching. I felt it in my gut. Shame and regret.

Where did that come from?

I hadn't hurt anyone.

Had I?

Well, yes, I had.

I'd opened a door to something that was desperate to get into my life and torment me.

I'd hurt myself.

Up to that point the 'secret place' had been something personal I had shared with God. I didn't know how much God and I had enjoyed in that place behind closed doors. It had just been defiled by the introduction of a parasite.

I'd hurt Him, too.

The 'secret place' is meant for you and God, it is meant to be a place of life-giving rest for you as a son or daughter. Because of a door that I had allowed to be opened, that 'secret place' was now suffering. I wanted help, I wanted to reach out to someone – my parents, or my brother, or my friend. Looking back now I know they would have helped me, but in that moment all I felt was shame and a compelling urge to lock it down and keep it hidden. I controlled my behaviour, learned to pretend nothing was wrong, kept my shame to myself and didn't invite anyone in to help me.

If what I'm saying rings true for you, if you've experienced something similar, know this before we go any further – Jesus' heart burns especially bright for those caught in the grip of a parasite trying to destroy them. Jesus sought out the ones carrying a burden of shame so He could lift it off of them. We'll get to that part, but first we have to go deeper into the problem.

Escalation

On mission trips to Kenya I have seen first-hand the effects of a parasitic flea called a 'jigger'. This is a particular nasty form of flea, just visible to the naked eye, which likes to live in dry, dusty environments. The jigger enters the fingernails and toenails of young children and the elderly, burrowing into the soft skin and growing to more than ten times its original size before it lays eggs spawning thousands of new jiggers. The result in the host is that their fingers and toes are slowly eaten away. Huge craters and bulbous sores remain in their place. It's utterly heartbreaking.

My wife returned home from a trip to Kenya unwittingly playing host to one of these in her toe for two weeks. It had to be gouged out with a needle and it was not pretty. What we thought was one adult jigger ended up being three. The look of pain and violation was wrought across my wife's face as they came out one after the other; the size of them, the way they had grown and were about to multiply… it was nasty. The degree to which the problem had escalated was shocking to both of us.

Sin escalates and grows the more it is given oxygen to breathe and space to live. I had my own experience of escalation in my area of struggle in the decade that followed. Glimpses of skin on a movie became active seeking out of adult, late-night movies. Late-night movies were trumped by the instant availability of images on the internet. Images gave way to videos. Soon I didn't even need to see something with my eyes, my brain having become very good at coming up with all kinds of imaginative things by itself. I didn't even need a device to provide something to feed the parasite.

One day at a church service, maybe I was sixteen or so, I went up to share at an open mic section meant for testimonies. I don't remember what I said but it was some small testimony about something I felt God had done and I had a chance to speak into a microphone, and my young heart longed for the platform. I approached the mic, shared, got a ripple of applause and then I retook my seat.

After the service, someone came up to me and said that while I was sharing the testimony, this person had had 'a word' that they believed was from God, and asked if I would like them to share it with me.

'Yes, of course,' I humbly said. I'll be honest, I thought this person was going to say that God had preaching for me in my future, that I was a great leader in the making, that people would one day hang on my every word. I was expecting a spiritual back rub. But the word that this person had for me was actually a single word: 'Masturbation.'

The moment it was said I felt the colour drain out of my face.

Not in a million years was I expecting to be called out like that. My mind went to a million places; I was in full-on panic mode. Over the months I had been in the church I was slowly building up a reputation in the youth group as a leader and as someone who was 'going for it'. Now my dirty laundry had just been presented to me by an elder in the church to my face. I could have denied it, but I fought against the instinct and admitted I had been struggling and said I'd like prayer.

The person who said this was very loving and kind, but I felt shame, I felt exposed and just desperately wanted to run out of the room. After praying for a few moments, I felt some peace and some forgiveness enter me. I was starting to feel better. I mean, it wasn't the way I would have chosen for it to happen, but maybe this was the break I needed to actually deal with this problem.

We were going to wrap it up when another member of the prayer team who was alongside us started to pray something over me. I can't remember most of what was said, but I know it was about keeping my eyes away from temptations, late-night TV, pornography, things on the internet and then, lastly, chat rooms.

I thought, 'Chat rooms? Why would he mention those?' I had never had any experience with them and had never even given them a second thought.

I left church and went home, licking my wounds, feeling a little loved, a lot ashamed and mainly relieved to have got through it.

Later that week I logged on to the computer and searched for chat rooms, curious to see why I had been warned off them. I suddenly saw pages upon pages of them, people pretending to be anyone they wanted, saying anything they wanted to each other. It was pretty harmless stuff, to be honest, like the playground chatter between friends at school. I went on a couple of times with some friends during a free time at my school; we were quite surprised that we could just meet someone from the other side of the world and chat. I made friends and found it to be pretty harmless.

I dipped my toe in.

I realised that I didn't need to actually put my own name up when I went in. I could pretend to be someone else, which felt kind of fun. Pretending felt almost natural; it was like all those games I used to play. We're going to be characters and we know this is just a game, right?

The problem was my ignorance of the increasing size of this once-little creature I had let land on my arm. I was now losing perspective on how it was escalating. Instead of channel hopping to find a glimpse of something on a movie, I could now go online and talk with someone and share any kind of fantasy I could think of. Everyone else had come on to these sites to do the same thing; it was the culture, and so it was easy to fall into it and be swept away by the current.

I'm talking around it, but the truth is, it was toxic and my soul was getting pounded each time. The occasional shame I had felt in my early teens had now become like a regular companion. Yet the rush I got each time I gave in was just enough to pull me back in again. Instead of coming into my bedroom and chatting with God, explaining a game to Him, whispering to Him as I lay in bed, I pursued this new outlet of make-believe fantasy.

The 'secret place' that was meant for Jesus, Father, Holy Spirit and I was now becoming a 'secret place' for me and this parasitic creature of sin to hide.

I was in trouble, and as before I didn't know who to share it with. I was afraid people would be disappointed in me and hurt that I hadn't shared my struggle with them, so I kept it from everyone. I was making friends in the church and starting to take my first steps into leadership, and foolishly, because I didn't want to threaten that, I didn't tell my leaders either.

By choosing to hold on to fear and control, I was limiting my options. My relationship with God and with those around me could have been the release valve to this pressure, but I was too scared to take the humble step and admit I needed help.

As I grew older in years and in the faith, even as I started stepping into places where I was seeing miracles, healings and signs and wonders happen with increasing frequency, I was still contending with this pressure behind closed doors. The definition of my 'secret place'[29] had been subverted. The name had been reassigned. It was still the 'secret place', but God had been forced out and replaced by this… thing. No one else was invited in.

I was hiding behind a tree like Adam and Eve,[30] avoiding God and not letting anyone who could have helped share the burden to see me. Tragically, all the people in my life, from family to friends and leaders would have been able to help me and love me through it. My orphan heart wasn't strong enough to risk trusting them, however, and so I struggled on alone.

I wasn't on my own, though; God the Father was looking out the window for me on the horizon and He was also standing with me in the freezing cold rain on the path of my brokenness.

Supernatural breakthrough?

I'm sharing my story here so you can engage with your own story and find hope where it has been misplaced or lost. God's Word shows us in more ways than I can relay here that a

---

[29] Psalm 31:20, NKJV
[30] Genesis 3:8.

relationship of trust with Him and with those around us is essential in releasing the grace we need to help us move out of the oppression and shame that a spiritual parasite can bring. His Word also shows us that breakthrough supernatural power can be released in a moment and change everything in an instant. In a simple summary, God does things through people and over time, and He does things in an instant and in power.

Many of us have experienced a moment when we hear that someone is sick and we have considered whether to pray for a miraculous healing, or pray that the peace of God comes and the medicine they are taking does its job. We have to ask ourselves if our faith is believing for those wonderful, big breakthrough moments, where everything that needs to happen occurs in a single moment of supernatural brilliance, or if our faith is more for the little drop-by-drop answer that comes over time – God's residing presence being with that person in their trial.

Some leaders, churches or theologies say that accountability, discipline, reading the Bible every day, as well as having checks and balances with people you trust and who can ask you the tough questions, will be the way to freedom. For others, the answer is found in prayer. Praying daily to have the strength to be pure, clean and free is the chosen method.

Other ministries, churches and theologies will say the answer will come in a moment of inner healing, or on a ministry impartation line, or through a single act of radical faith. Praying for someone with an expectation that the power of God will fall in that exact moment and do something extraordinary.

Many people will find themselves in one of these camps, and some will bounce back and forth between the two.

I believe we need to have faith for *both*.

Ultimately, when we are seeking our breakthrough or someone else's, we need to be doing what God has told us to do, even if it's not what we would normally do. Jesus healed one person of paralysis by commanding Him to get up and another of blindness by wiping mud in their eyes. For Him it wasn't

101

about a formula, it was about doing what the Father was saying to do.[31]

I would say my experience has led me to realise we need to draw from both extremes of the theological spectrum, as the Holy Spirit leads. I am learning that finding a complementary balance of the two is what is really needed: grace for the long haul with Jesus and expectation for an immediate move of God's Spirit. The relational trust element and the supernatural miracle moment. Good spiritual disciplines and yielding to the Spirit of power. Long-term accountability and immediate deliverance.

Some moments may feel like physiotherapy and others like surgery.

In my story, for a long time I was only pursuing a supernatural breakthrough moment of healing and freedom in my struggle. If I'm honest, I'd given up on the accountability thing. I felt it wasn't working. I wanted desperately just to go up to a prayer line one day and to come back completely free of the need for false comforts. It seemed like a reasonable thing to ask for; it *had* worked for me once before, after all.

I used to struggle with alcohol: it wasn't pretty. I had been dipping cautiously, exploring it from about the age of seventeen, but it was my first year of university where everything just unravelled. I was trying to be a good Christian and share about Jesus with people in my halls of residence, but I was also getting blind drunk with them each night in the pubs and clubs. Drunkenly trying to share the gospel at a bar in a club was not a strong moment for me, but I just couldn't seem to rein it in. I was hating the person I became when I was under the influence. One weekend, though, in my second year of university, by an act of grace, God completely and utterly plucked this reliance on alcohol out of my life.

It was simply a supernatural miracle. I can't really tell you what He did, other than that one day He got my butt back in

---

[31] Luke 5:24; John 9:6-7; John 5:19.

church and put His Spirit in me afresh in a way that somehow just seemed to crowd out the desire to drink. I can't explain it; *it just happened.* In the seventeen years since that weekend, alcohol has not been a problem for me. I love having fun with my friends, I still enjoy a glass of wine or a cold beer, but I don't even remotely miss being drunk. I'm so grateful to God that He just *dealt with it.*

So if a reliance on alcohol bordering on addiction could be lifted out of me in a weekend, surely I could expect the same thing to happen with another addictive problem? Isn't that an expectation you can have for your life and those parasites that are trying to embed themselves in you?

Well, just like lust, gambling or body image management, to name a few, alcohol invades the 'secret place' for many people. It calls to them as they walk on the road to the Father's house and leads them to willingly walk off the road into the tall grass and all the snares and thorns it hides. It is toxic. However, what I realised was that alcohol was a source of shame for me, *but it wasn't the deepest source.* There was a parasite trying to dig into my skin there, but it wasn't as embedded as the other one. Maybe this was why God could sovereignly remove the need for alcohol and the whole culture surrounding drinking from me.

I want to be careful not to build a whole theology on this thought, but it became clear to me that the deeper issues required God to go deeper still. He can decide to move sovereignly, but He is a God of relationship and proved through Abraham, Moses and many others that He is willing to go the long way round with us. You may want a sovereign act, but He may want your character to mature.

As I looked on my struggle with false comforts, in my heart I just wanted to take a shortcut. I wanted an easy way out. I wanted God to do it for me. I didn't want a slow path of obedience, and I didn't want to have to trust God daily for the strength to resist what I'd allowed to become habit. I wanted Him to do what He had done with the alcohol. I just wanted it lifted up and out of me in a weekend. I wanted a sovereign act of deliverance, not an invitation to a lifetime of trust. I sought out a solution in self-control strategies and in the inner healing prayer room, looking for each one to provide 'the fix'. I wanted the breakthrough so much but I didn't know what I was asking for. *The healing God gave me became the story at the heart of this book.* It was all about a daily walk with God, trusting Him and others with me and my journey.

Some of that healing involves praying. Some of it involves talking. Some of it involves being very wise with my thought life and using common sense. A lot of it involves recognising that God is looking to be part of my solution, my greatest encourager, not some mean teacher at their desk at the front of class waiting for me to bring my homework up at the end of the lesson for grading.

I'm grateful that God interprets our prayers for us. In this case I'm really glad God didn't lift off *desire* from me, because I actually quite like being attracted to my wife, desiring her and being married to her. God always knows better. That may be something to remind yourself of right now if you are trying to see your breakthrough come, like I was. Realising where we have made idols of *how* we think things should be done is where we are going next.

That's not what I asked for, God

Whether it is owing to our familiarity with stories from the Bible or because we have latched on to someone else's testimony, we can very easily find ourselves in a trap where we have unwittingly made an idol about *how* things should be done. When it comes to our breakthrough, healing and freedom, we do this all the time, and to be honest, I think it ends up becoming a blockage to the very thing we were hoping for. Here are some examples of God providing in ways that weren't expected:

- In Exodus 16, the Israelites in the wilderness reminded Moses about the 'meat pots' (v3) they used to have when they were slaves in Egypt. God saw their need and heard their cry and gave them little flakes of manna on the ground to collect each day, one day at a time, that could be baked into cakes, as well as quail in the evening. God's provision lasted forty years.

- In 1 Samuel 16, the prophet was led to anoint a new king to replace Saul. He was expecting everything you expect a king to look like. He had his checklist in his head ready to be completed upon setting eyes on the new king. What he got was some kid. The kid wasn't even deemed important enough to make the first round of potentials. This kid, David, grew to become the greatest king the nation had ever known.

- Lastly, the greatest example I can think of. The cross. *The cross was no one's idea of provision.* It wasn't on anyone's list as the potential source of a breakthrough over sin. It was so far removed from the idea of liberation that it was no wonder the disciples thought the movement had ended the moment Jesus was lifted up on it. The world needed a breakthrough and what it got was a thirty-three-year-old man nailed to a tree until his life gave out. Yet, more than two thousand years later, people wear this torture device on necklaces. People see this sign as the greatest symbol of hope and liberation the world has ever known. Even those who don't hold faith in Jesus respect the symbol. It's holy.

God provides and so often it doesn't look the way we want it to, nor even like what we've asked Him for. Yet it's always what we need.

The freed Israelites were looking for the food of their former captivity, the prophet of the nation was looking for a king who looked like the one he was seeking to replace, and Jewish people of the first century were looking for a military king to defeat the military power that was oppressing them. God confounded their expectations, and confounds our expectations, every time.

We need to be very careful that we do not dictate to God how He should provide for us. 'Prayer and supplication' are biblical (Ephesians 6:18; Philippians 4:6), but giving God an ultimatum that your healing or breakthrough needs to come like you saw it come for someone else, or like you'd prefer it to come, well, that may not get you very far.

Despite much hunger and desperation for 'my moment' of breakthrough, the Father had something different in mind. He had me on a daily journey of trust. He still does to this day. As I walk my own road to the Father's house, I walk through the woodlands and see in my periphery the other ways, the shortcuts, the easy ways out I could take, and the straight, narrow road ahead to where I want to get to. I still have to choose the straight and narrow way; I just know now, more than ever, He is by my side when I'm making the choice.

The more I have sought Him the more I have found Him, and the more I have encountered Him the more I have found my needs met in Him. God has provision for us, but the way we access it is by taking up the daily invitation offered by the Father to seek Him and choose Him before choosing what we need from Him. Each day I choose Him in the 'secret place', I replace one of those days when I didn't. I reclaim the ground with each choice to trust His nearness, whether I feel it or not.

We need the supernatural and the relational elements to our healing journey, but ultimately we need to cultivate an intimacy with God where we just know His voice better than we did the day before. I started to realise that sometimes He was helping me with my struggles through the counsel of a good friend, other days He was helping me by putting a fire in my belly during a moment of worship, and other days it was a word from the Bible jumping off the page at 8am on a Monday morning before work.

God the Father, Son and Holy Spirit is full of love and grace, but He knows how destructive idols are in our lives (just read 1 and 2 Kings for further evidence of this). He wants to help us bring them down and see us free of them. That then clears the ground for His intervention in our lives... however and whenever He chooses to do it.

God doesn't do shame and He doesn't do waste

As I close this chapter I want to say something about my not-so-great encounter at church as a teenager. Someone gave me that word about masturbation, and even though it was tough to hear and experience, I knew it came from a place of love and wanting to see me free of something that was toxic in my life. In the moment, however, the result of the word given to me was that I became terrified of God. 'God could see what I did in private and if I didn't own up... well, He would expose me and He'd tell someone about it.'

I want to speak to anyone who has this fear. Let me tell you clearly here: God is not out to get you. Romans 8:1 says clearly, 'There is therefore now no condemnation for those who are in Christ Jesus.'

There is no punishment, sentencing, rejection for those who belong to Messiah Jesus.

God doesn't do shame.

Even though my heart didn't receive it well in the moment, I still needed to hear that word. The enemy jumped on the back of the moment and allowed the word to open up a fear that God was going to expose my sins to others. For years after that I was scared of getting a prophetic word. I was convinced it was going to happen again. Any time prophetic words were being given in church from the front, I'd do anything I could to avoid eye contact with the person doing it. The idea of having my sins and bad choices detailed to the whole church was terrifying.

The enemy sought to use what had happened to get me to fear God and escalate me to a worse kind of sin, believing God is someone He is not, and then living my life based on that lie.

107

I had to repent of believing that He was the kind of Father who would set out to expose His children.

He's not. He's a good God and a He's good Father.

Instead, in the words of Paul Manwaring, 'he wastes nothing and he gets you ready'.[32]

That day was not wasted in my life. Your experiences of days like that are not wasted either. I have a deep level of compassion for anyone caught in secret sin, trapped in something they don't feel they can share with anyone. I know what it feels like and I feel the Father's love gushing out of me to anyone in that place.

I want to be really clear to anyone who has picked up this book because they feel their 'secret place' has become overrun by darkness. Let me tell you this:

- First, the Father loves you with a rich, longing love, even in what feels like your worst moments. He loves you deeply and with great strength. Even if you have wandered off the road and are on your knees, off the path, and with a thorny vine tightly coiled around your legs, He sees you and loves you.

- Second, He is capable of getting you out of it. He is strong enough to break the back of that thing, to snap the thorny vine or to lift you out of it. You and I try so hard to get ourselves out of the traps we have been snared in. He is able. Take a moment to remind yourself of that and let it settle.

- Third, it will not be wasted.

- He will make your rescue and rehabilitation the foundations upon which a testimony of freedom will be built, if you'll let Him. Even if it takes a daily choosing to

---

[32] paulmanwaring.com/2016/02/08/he-wastes-nothing-he-gets-you-ready (accessed 8th February 2016). Used with permission.

devote the 'secret place' and your behind-the-scenes life to Him and not an illicit pleasure, He'll see you through.

Placing real trust in God and in others who know Him gives me the chance to step into a warm and welcoming light where the most shameful parts of me can be known and seen... and yet I am so deeply loved in sharing them

> Jesus stood up and said to her, 'Woman, where are [those who accused you]? Has no one condemned you?' She said, 'No one, Lord.' And Jesus said, 'Neither do I condemn you; go, and from now on sin no more.'
> (John 8:10-11)

7
Communicate

When your Father crashed into you on that path, there was a moment where every muscle in your being tensed up. For a moment your body was preparing for an attack, a beating. Punishment for sin, or a reprimand for not doing well enough. Whatever conditioning by religion or family or experiences you may have had, there was a moment (and that moment could have lasted seconds or decades) when you were braced for judgement.

It never came. You got mercy. You got grace.

The Father came over the hill, down the road from His house onto the path you were walking and careered into you with a hug so powerful your knees buckled under you. With it came laughter, crying and a gut-wrenching sound as your grief and relief and the Father's compassionate heart collided.

For some sons and daughters, when they think of that moment with the Father, it really was 'a moment'. They were on their knees weeping when it came, in a church or on their bedroom floor; it all happened in a few minutes when all the pain and the striving of the years felt like it was wiped away and replaced with His goodness. For others there was no single 'moment'. The hug of the Father was felt gradually, slowly, consistently over many months and years. It was rich and deep, and the more they trusted, the more it landed.

There was another significant moment that was part of the story, one that can sometimes be forgotten in the euphoria of remembering your

Dad's love that day. It was, however, a moment that had a lot of significance to it.

The apology. Or the repentance. Or maybe just the moment when something that needed to be said was said: 'God... I really messed up. I knew what the right thing to do was; and then I did exactly the opposite of that... in fact, I couldn't have gone harder or more foolishly into the wrong thing if I had tried. I hurt You, I know I did, you're my Dad and You've always loved me and cared for me. You've provided everything I've ever owned or needed, and somehow I managed to forget all that and mess up. I didn't trip or stumble or do this by accident. I chose to do this... please forgive me.'

Communicating this was good; it was needed. It would also have been a great moment to take a breath, to pause and let Him respond, but everything was tumbling out of your mouth. You knew that you had not acted like the child you were, and you knew that something needed to be done about that. You had to seek the demotion, ask to be benched, drop your rank or title or something... there was no way you were going to be able to return to that exact place of being a child again. You just needed to get out ahead of it, speak the words out, do what needed to be done.

'Dad, I...'

'I'm going to stop you there,' He says, kindly but firmly.

A hand on your shoulder, leaning in, eye-to-eye contact; this all should have been uncomfortable but somehow you were able to hold His gaze, almost as if He were giving you the ability to do so.

'You're My child. Do you understand?'

'Yes, but...'

'My child.'

And then He smiled, and the rest was a blur. Waves of love, affirmation, force of life and fire washed over you.

On the dirt path under the hot afternoon sun, the Father picked you up off the ground in His hug and held you close. That was the moment you owned up to it all, and also the moment you tried to make His job easier and lower your status and place before Him. He just wouldn't let you.

Repenting, confessing and expressing words of sorrow when we have messed it all up and got it wrong isn't easy, enjoyable or appealing. To be honest, I have spent significant portions of my life trying to escape doing it or getting around it somehow.

Speaking to our mistakes, our poor choices and owning the decisions we have made is an important part of our sonship journey; we can't really take a shortcut around it, even if we'd like to. It's one of the things that helps us turn and start going in the right direction. The younger son in the parable realised this when he made up his mind to return home to His Father. In Luke 15:18-19 he says this to himself: 'I will arise and go to my father, and I will say to him, "Father, I have sinned against heaven and before you. I am no longer worthy to be called your son. Treat me as one of your hired servants."'

There are two ways we could think about this part of the story soteriologically from our twenty-first-century perspective. First, we could suggest that the younger son had never been 'saved', and therefore, when he goes back and meets the father (who is God) and confesses his sin, he is forgiven and restored and made new. We can see him as a person without faith, realising that God's saving power is needed, then inviting Him in and asking Him to clear away all his brokenness and sin. This viewpoint works. Theologically it is sound. If you're a Jesus follower, you did this at some point. I hope and pray it changed your life. If you're not a Jesus follower, I hope one day soon you'll have this experience.

The second way we could view this part of the story is to suggest that the boy was already a redeemed son, a saved person, but one who had lost his way and made some bad choices that caused him to flee from God his Father. He realises his mistakes, he repents of those things and that way of thinking and turns back. He too gets met by the embrace of the Father, forgiven and restored.

There's not a single Christian on the planet who hasn't made a selfish choice or a decision to let evil desires, or greed of some kind or another, get the better of them. God forgives and covers all this with His grace. So this second way of viewing the story works for me too, but let me expand a little on it.

When I was younger I wondered about this parable as I tried to get my head round the theology of it. I had a lot of questions: 'Was the son getting re-saved? Does that mean I experience salvation again when I come back after wandering or sinning? Am I really a saved person if I go and sin again? What does God need me to say or do when I've messed up; how do I make it right?'

My background was in high Church Anglo-Catholicism and then my formative years were spent in the evangelical movement. Both streams have a different perspective on sin, confession and repentance. I was pretty confused as a teenager, to be honest; so the above were questions I just didn't have answers to.

The cross was and is God's one response to the sin of humankind. We don't need to, nor can we, re-crucify Jesus for our sins when we mess up. We don't need to be re-saved. All our sin was accounted for on that day – past, present and future. As the prophet Zechariah said, hundreds of years before Jesus died at Calvary: '[God] will remove the iniquity of this land in a single day' (Zechariah 3:9). And He did.

The cross is enough for all of us.

This prodigal son story works as an evangelistic story, but it also works as a relational one for believers, asking the question of what happens between us and God when our orphan behaviour rears its head again. We have a connection with Him as saved, redeemed children, but we still have the ability to put blockages and barriers between us and Him. The sin that has cut us off from God has been addressed by Jesus on the cross, so these subsequent blockages don't separate us from Him or discount our salvation, but like the dirt on the disciples' feet that Jesus washed off,[33] they need to be addressed. They affect our relationship with Him.

---

[33] John 13:1-20.

We are totally useless at removing the effects and consequences of sin, no matter how hard we try. It's like putting toothpaste back in a tube: we're perfectly capable of getting it out in the first place but incapable of putting it back in. It is the grace of Jesus that comes to us, His presence in our lives, standing beside us, clearing away the rubble of the cave-in we have caused, that deals with it.

We cannot do what only God can do. However, there are moments where an opportunity to grow, mature and step into a deeper level of sonship arise. These are opportunities to repent, to say sorry and to admit that we came careering off the track and flipped the car of our lives on its roof because we just weren't making good choices. The son in Luke 15 understood this thought – *almost*.

His confession is very interestingly worded. He admits his sin, which is a good thing, and he recognises his choices have caused harm against the Father's heart, and even the heavens, the dominion of God. He even recognises that sin stains and taints and should disqualify us from being sons and daughters of God. This is where it gets especially interesting. Let's pick up the story in verse 20:

> And he arose and came to his father. But while he was still a long way off, his father saw him and felt compassion, and ran and embraced him and kissed him. And the son said to him, 'Father, I have sinned against heaven and before you. I am no longer worthy to be called your son.' But the father said to his servants, 'Bring quickly the best robe, and put it on him, and put a ring on his hand, and shoes on his feet. And bring the fattened calf and kill it, and let us eat and celebrate. For this my son was dead, and is alive again; he was lost, and is found.' And they began to celebrate.
> (vv20-24)

The son gets two-thirds of the way through his apology. He doesn't get to finish it, though.

- The son is able to acknowledge he sinned.

- He recognises that his sin was against the Father and heaven.

- He is also able to acknowledge that this sin should disqualify him.

However, *he is not able to say* that he should be treated as one of the Father's 'hired servants'; the Father won't let him get the sentence out.

He may feel wretched, he may feel he deserves a demotion, he may even have theological evidence for it, but his father won't even let it be spoken. The father won't allow it because it's not his present reality, nor is it his future destiny. This son of his has come back to life. The ring of authority, the seal upon which gives him the ability to pay for things with his father's resources, is put on his finger. The filth and the stain of his impurity is covered by the best robes. And the fattened calf, the best meat in the house, is immediately prepared, as if a royal guest was coming to visit. The son is a *full* son again.

Now, the son was allowed to say *something*, don't miss that point. Jesus was deliberate with His words. The son did say sorry. He had hurt the father, though that hurt couldn't extinguish the father's love, mercy and grace towards him and it couldn't stop the father releasing forgiveness.

The son wanted to honour his father. He wanted to make it right, even if there was very little he could do to actually achieve that. He acknowledged what had happened. He took ownership over his part in it all. He chose to step into the maturity he lacked earlier in the story, and confessed where he just got it wrong. Taking this step, saying those words and meaning them was like a love gift to his dad. This wasn't some religious statement; this was his heart giving the only thing it had left to give.

We cannot save ourselves, nor can we apologise ourselves out of our sin. We cannot remove sin from our lives by any means other than the cross of Christ, and when we choose the cross, it is God doing the fixing work, not us.

We can, however, offer a love gift to our Father, to God, when we've messed up and missed the mark. We can honour our relationship and repent, say sorry, confess, knowing that we haven't lost our salvation, nor do we need Jesus to re-crucify Himself. This is part of what being a son and a daughter of God is about. It's not about living in what Dietrich Bonhoeffer called 'cheap grace'[34] but instead about honouring costly grace. I believe repenting to God for our sin, as Christians, is a right thing to do. We are still on the journey of sanctification, and although our sin cannot overpower the blood of Christ in us and on us, it can still grieve Him, and we can come to Him and own it.

The beauty of it is that even before we have been able to own those mistakes we've made, the Father has seen us coming on the horizon. Before we know it He is running like the wind, landing upon us so strongly that our knees buckle at the weight of His embrace. He covers us with kisses, presses His heart of compassion against our weak heart and pours love into us. He actually empowers us to be able to 'walk in the light'.[35] We're only really able to do so because He makes us able to and because He's already forgiven us, and is already standing beside us.

God just won't let us reduce ourselves in His eyes. He calls every returning, repenting, turning-back child of His exactly that – a child.

[34] Dietrich Bonhoeffer, *The Cost of Discipleship* (New York: Touchstone, 1995).
[35] 1 John 1:5-7.

Not your shame story

My friend Vic Woodward said: 'You are not your shame story.'[36] Maybe you need to hear that right now. Maybe you need to hear that for yourself and store it in your back pocket for someone else to hear one day. When we believe we are our shame story, we won't share with anyone when we are struggling; we get locked down and isolated inside our own heads, and we slowly veer off the road to God and loop round until we rejoin the old familiar path where we tried to do it all ourselves. This isn't the Father's heart for us.

God doesn't take sin lightly, but He loves sinners. Jesus was accused of dining with the sinners of society, including the rejected and hated tax collectors.[37] He talked to prostitutes and promiscuous spouses. He touched people with skin diseases considered contagious and unclean. He stepped over the threshold of people's lives and pushed past their shame story to get to the real them hidden inside.

These stories give me hope that Jesus isn't repulsed or disgusted by our shame. These stories remind me that He can ride into the middle of our struggles and bring the decisive victory or healing we need.

Now, as already shared, we need to make sure that even biblical stories don't become unintentional idols for us when we are looking for our moment of healing. It is very easy to find ourselves wanting someone else's 'freedom moment'. We want the way it worked out for that friend, or that preacher, or that person who wrote that inspiring book to be the way it works out for us. Sometimes we even replicate the things they did to try to get the same result. I'm not knocking being inspired by someone's testimony of freedom, but I am highlighting the need

---

[36] Vic Woodward, used with permission, www.buzz-sprout.com/42863/4864238-vic-and-monique-woodward-living-in-holi-ness-is-living-with-nothing-hidden (accessed 7th July 2021).
[37] Matthew 9:11.

to own our journey and the road to freedom and out of shame God will offer us each individually.

I have paid attention to people's testimonies over the years, listening out for the part of the story where there would be that inevitable mic-dropping moment as they shared how God brought the breakthrough, the redemptive answer and it all got fixed. It's so compelling to hear someone share their 'road to Damascus experience'[38] that 'fixed' the problem and took away the shame. As I have grown older and more mature in the faith, however, I have come to realise that there are as many slow miracle stories as there are fast, instantaneous ones. Now, we have to learn to celebrate them both, even if we would prefer the quick supernatural ones. God is deeply concerned with our character and, for many of us, breakthrough and freedom will be dependent on our choosing to trust God with what we're feeling and to live free one day at a time. Moment by moment.[39]

When everything has been fine for weeks and then one day temptation arises and we feel dejected, like we should have been free of this by now, we remind ourselves that we are a redeemed child of God and we're not handling this on our own.

Whenever a reminder of that shame that we've longed to move on from presents itself out of the blue again, we make a fresh choice in that moment to believe we are not our shame story but God's redemption testimony.

When the enemy starts digging, or the parasite reappears and tries to infiltrate again, we maturely remember that we can't just rely on a choice we made months or years ago to believe God. We choose again that day, in that moment, to be the saved and free child of the Father we truly are.

If God does it all in a moment and supernaturally frees you of all future struggle, then hallelujah, that is amazing. Share your story, encourage us all – we'll be celebrating with you. But if you have to choose to be free one day at a time, don't discount that

---

38 Acts 9:1-19.
39 Romans 5:3-5; Galatians 5:22-23; 6:8-9; 1 Timothy 4:12.

as a move of God, don't say it's invalid. He is building your character. He's girding you up for the future. He's strengthening you to be able to walk into incredible things down the line. Your story is yours, not someone else's. The Father loves all His children and He treats them all individually.

When Philippians 2:12 talks about working out our salvation 'with fear and trembling', one of the things it means is to allow God to have His place in the daily process of living our lives. Not like a friend who comes over for weekends and sleeps in the guest room, but as a permanent member of the household. Choosing to give God permanent residence allows Him to help with the stuff we can't cope with by ourselves.

Being honest about our struggles, walking as 'children of light',[40] is not an easy thing to do for most of us. Living free is living without any skeletons in the closet, but for so many of us we've learned that sharing our sin or our mistakes leads to rejection more than it leads to healing, and so we've just stopped doing it. The spiritual orphan mindset compensates for this by holding others at a distance, protecting you from further pain. It works at locking things down but it also means that you can never enjoy living in the light; it's too costly to ever be a viable option.

As sons and daughters of the Father, you and I don't have to be our shame story. We don't need to be our struggle story. We don't need to put a Christian face on and look like we've got this thing covered when we absolutely do not.

Jesus, the ultimate and perfect Son, modelled sonship to us all. He had friends. He had people to walk with, and on the night before His worst day He honestly told His friends how He was doing, just as He told His Father in heaven too. In the Garden of Gethsemane, Jesus knelt before God and experienced the supernatural strengthening and the presence of God landing on Him, but He also asked His friends to stay awake with Him and

---

[40] Ephesians 5:8.

keep Him company.[41] You and I, as sons and daughters, need to do the same. We have to be honest before God and before people when things are getting tough; we have to reverse out of any alleyways of shame we've driven down, even if it's slow and there's only one gear.

As I started to open up about my struggles, began to share in small groups, with the mentors, I had to look a few people in the eye and say a bunch of stuff I'd really rather have kept to myself. I had to 'walk in the light'. Most of the time it was really freeing. Sometimes it was super-awkward because the other person didn't know what to do with it. It has always been good and right, though, to step into the light. The fruit of it is always freedom in your heart. That is worth something.

'The light' should be somewhere we actually choose to live in, rather than just occasionally step into. That's what the walk to the Father's house is for: the closer we get to our true home in Him, the lighter it gets. Living in the light with God and others is not easy or comfortable, but doing it will be the unravelling of your shame story and mine.

The first step into all this is learning to be real and authentic before God. The next step is sharing the real us with people filled with the love of God, who will be able to look past our shame and see that hurt and wounded little boy or little girl behind the self-created armour. Not everyone in your life is going to be one of those people. You might have to search for those grace-filled people and pray for them to come into your life if you don't already have them around you. You will need them to communicate with, relate with and journey with. They will need you too.

Foxes and fences

In Song of Songs chapter 2, the poetry depicts a love story of pursuit between a man and a woman, helping us to understand

---

41 Matthew 26:38.

the love story of pursuit between God and us. The lovers are tripping over themselves to talk about how much they desire each other, as they dote on, woo, yearn for and contend for each other. Then suddenly in verse 15 we take a complete U-turn into garden maintenance:

> Catch the foxes for us,
> the little foxes
> that spoil the vineyards,
> for our vineyards are in blossom.

Why would a love poem be interrupted by a request to remove foxes from a vineyard? It seems like two pages have been turned over at once, taking us from a moment of romance to the next thing on the 'to-do' list. If I were an editor of the book of Song of Songs, I might circle this part in red and say 'consider moving this to later in the book, tonally jarring'. The reason for its inclusion is relatively simple, however; the 'little foxes' are the things that appear to be minor pests at first, but over time devour your resources, your supplies, the very things you have been growing to enjoy with your lover.

Even in the moments of romance and intimacy with your beloved, this verse shows that we need our radar activated for these pests and the influence they can have. Not only are we to be aware of them, but also we need to be communicating about them.

The 'little foxes' will destroy all that you have worked so hard to build up and they have to be dealt with. Fences need to be put up and they will need to be maintained. The holes must be found and repaired. You might be growing a beautiful vineyard of intimacy with God and those in your life, but the three-piece suit or ball gown will need to come off and be replaced with overalls, boots and gloves so you can get down in the dirt and make the borders secure. It is hard work and it can't just be done once in our life. The repairs, the walls, the fences: it will all need to be watched and kept over time. Advice will need to be sought.

Getting some experts to come in and test the strength of the fence you erect might be required too.

Doing all this may well earn you the reputation of a strict conservative who is out of touch with reality and culture, maybe someone who is overly fussy, or stuck in traditional ways of doing things, and out of touch. Doing these things may also be exactly what is needed to protect the most important thing in your life.

Boundaries protect something. You don't have a boundary unless you are seeking to protect something. 'Boundaries protect valuable things; they protect values'.[42]

We put a fence around something important: a building, a statue, a home, even a piece of empty land if it is being set apart for something. We choose to put in this effort because valuable things need protecting to keep their value. In this life journey of stepping out of orphanness into sonship, we must know what we are protecting and why it is worth contending for. 'Trying to be a better Christian' is just not a sufficient motivator to protect something this precious.

Psalm 34:8 invites us to first taste and then see that God is good. The simple inference being that we don't get the revelation that God is good before we have experienced that He is good. We taste His goodness *first* – then we realise He's everything He says He is, and *that* is what makes us hungry for more.

When we taste the living water, the wine, the bread, the sweet honey, the oil, the body and the blood of God Himself, we get hungry for more of Him. Each day that we 'taste and see' a bit more of Him than the day before, we start to make the main thing the main thing. He becomes our greatest value, and what we have with Him becomes the thing we want to protect above all.

The more we value the presence of God in our life, the less patience we have for those little creatures that try to hang on,

---

[42] Tom Allsop. Used with permission.

and the more understanding we have for the need of good boundaries. We don't take off our armour to accommodate the parasitic pet. We don't leave a gap for the foxes to enter in. We stop being silent or weaving tales to hide how we're really doing. We don't try to spray air freshener over the smell of decay when someone comes into our world and asks how we're really doing. The right thing to do becomes wisdom rather than obligation.

Our intimacy with God drives our honesty with others. The orphan-hearted son in the parable found his honesty in the pigsty of his mistakes, but the courage to be vulnerable came after he experienced his father's embrace. As we 'taste and see' that God is good more and more each day and as we trust that we really are His adopted children, we too find the courage to be vulnerable and honest with God and others.

Now, from my experience, living like this takes time. My heart, my habits, my thinking require time to change. Sometimes the best you can offer when someone asks you how your freedom journey is going is to say that you have chosen to be free right now, and with God's strength and the Holy Spirit you are going to be free for the rest of the day. Sometimes that's enough. It doesn't need to look or sound impressive. It just needs to be real.

So some questions at this point would be:

- Do you know what core values you have that need to be protected?

- How do you feel about sharing with someone else your journey (successes and failures) of protecting those values?

- What support do you need from God and others to be able to live a day-to-day life where the most important thing is kept safe and pure?

For some of us, our journey out of the orphan lifestyle means coming out of a place of controlling and fixing things on our own, without anyone else's help. We may also be spending a lot of time thinking about our boundaries and the next thing on the list that needs to be done to secure them, entirely forgetting that those fences are there to protect what is on the inside – something that we are actually meant to be enjoying. The older son in the story had lost sight of this very thing.

There may be some heart work to be done here. Open and honest conversations with your spouse, mentor, small group members or friends may need to happen. You may need to sit down with wise and godly people and talk about the repairs that are needed in your fences and walls. You may need to place yourself around people who are so consumed with Jesus and His kingdom that you too can remember what the main thing is meant to be.

In my life, I am finding that it is much wiser to be humble and talk to someone about a little fox that is making a small hole in my fence. Trying to pretend that everything is fine even though the whole vineyard is being overrun behind my back doesn't seem to help anyone in the long run. Keep communicating.

Turning and thinking

When the son in the parable repents to his Father and says that he sinned, the Greek word the Bible uses for 'sin' is *hamartano*. It means 'to have missed the mark'. The word speaks to loss, not being in the flow of God's perfect will, choosing instead to be in the flow of our own will and desires. Simply put, it is just getting things completely wrong in every possible way.

There are multiple words in the New Testament used for repentance, most of which at their root have a different meaning than just 'confessing and saying sorry', which is an unfortunate modern-day misunderstanding of the meaning. Two words in particular are used in the New Testament for repentance and they describe two very particular actions: turning and thinking.

The Greek word used in Acts 3:19 is *epistrepho*, which means to turn around and head away from the direction you were going in and go in a new, better direction. The other Greek word, *metanoeo* (Acts 11:18; Romans 2:4), means to change your mind and think differently. It's about amending your thought patterns from whatever form they used to take to something new and better.

So repentance is *turning and walking in a new direction* (or perhaps revisiting and walking the good, 'ancient paths' that are proven to get you where you need to be, Jeremiah 6:16) and it is *changing how we think* (using 'the mind of Christ', 1 Corinthians 2:16).

Everything we have spoken about in these last two chapters is about these two things. Turning back to where and Whom we came from, and changing the way we think, moving past the old, defunct way of making decisions and how we think about ourselves, or how we deal with our problems.

Each one of these 'acts of repentance' leads us back to Him.

I don't know what pain you have in your history, or what issues you have been churning over in your mind as you have been reading this. Secret sin, past mistakes, decisions made in fear or haste, isolation. It could be all or none of those. Time and time again, God's Word calls us to take hope and remember there is a way back for all who seek it. For all who take it, there is an empowerment to walk in that new direction and to think in a new way.

We often fail because we try to tick religious boxes to get ourselves out of trouble. We try to communicate to God or others in a way we feel we are expected to, rather than just from our hearts, which is all God is looking for.

The 'right thing to do' in God's eyes is also 'the empowered thing to do'. Every one of the steps we need to take is pre-resourced by the Holy Spirit in our lives. So when we 'walk in the light' with those around us and go back and do what we 'did at first' before everything blew up,[43] we don't do it alone; we do it fuelled by the Holy Spirit in us and on us. Each step along the way, when we do the right thing, make the right choice, own up

---

[43] James 5:16; Revelation 2:5.

to the stuff and turn away from the trash, we do it with our new, 'Christ in [me]' [44] nature front and centre. Each course adjustment and course correction slowly starts to refocus us towards Him rather than away from Him.

If sin is about missing the mark and going in the wrong direction, repentance is about turning away from that wrong direction and thinking in a new 'mark-hitting' kind of way. From that place we can look forward to the walk home to the Father's house and the life we will live from it. We don't need to have fear that the moment we make a mistake we will be demoted or disowned.

Coming out of a lifestyle that had sinful patterns and habits can be a slow process for many. I wish it wasn't, but it's just the way it is when you are a human and still a work in progress. The grace collision on the prodigal path is the moment you and I were renewed and made into a new creature that we weren't before. Our shame story was obliterated in that moment. A new relationship with God the Father and God the universe builder was birthed. The walk home, though, is the rest of our lives and that means we still have many more moments ahead of us to share, to be authentic and to allow Him to shape our thinking and adjust our heading.

God loves trust and He loves authentic living. He also loves His children to understand that they *are* His children now, no matter what. Like the son on the road, He will let us share what we need to share so we can turn and face the right direction once again. The Father just won't let one of His children try to convince Him they are no longer His child. He's too loving to let us do that.

---

[44] Colossians 1:27.

8
Two Trenches

You had been walking for about an hour. Shoulder to shoulder, side by side along that path with the Father. The path was still stony and sandy, but you felt more assured with Him by your side.

It was and is a strange experience, walking with God. You knew this wasn't a normal afternoon walk two people were sharing, no matter what it looked like from the outside looking in. Under the cloak you were wearing, you were still dirty and covered in sores and needed washing, tending and time to heal. Your wrist had been hurting for some time; you may have fractured it, you weren't sure, but it didn't feel right. The dried mud around your ankles, caked like a sealant around your skin, was hard to shake, even if it was covered by the new cloak. Those nights out in the dark and the rain, stumbling in potholes, felt like a blurred memory as you were walking but their impact was still evident on you. Despite all this, right there and then you were covered and you were safe. You were even laughing again.

The ring on your finger was catching the sunlight and the glow of your Dad. The robe, with its warm colours – rich, deep reds – covered everything from your neck down to your feet. And then there were those shoes, beautiful leather, comfortable and secure.

You were covered and restored, but there was still some washing and wound-tending to come.

As you walked past people, however, all they saw was someone covered in finery and security. Someone with their Father's arm around their waist. A child, and not an orphan. A person with a destiny, not a project with issues.

So you walked and He listened to your thoughts and your questions and His answers flowed through you in different ways. It was hard to describe the conversation, but it was a conversation. You were talking about the entirety of your life, all your choices and decisions, and then a moment later you were talking about the flowers in the field you were passing. It was all 'big picture' and then all 'immediate'.

After maybe a mile of this, something started to distract you. You stopped in the road for a moment as it stretched out ahead; the soft gravel was giving way to a harder clay surface, and a long straight with two fields lay either side of it. You knew a little further on it would become stone, then cobbled flagstone and then something more precious.

You had walked down this road when you left His house the first time. You didn't notice a single detail about it then; it was dark and your mind just wasn't in a place to notice things that weren't about you. You were thinking about what you wanted and where you were going, that city in the far-off land that you were heading towards.

Before you, on the left and on the right of the road, there were deep slopes down.

Two trenches.

They looked easy to fall into. Very steep. Hard to get out of.

In one of them, the left one, there were what looked like steps descending down, but they were broken, leaving sharp flint and brittle rocks on their surfaces. Severe edges of unforgiving granite and stone all the way down to the bottom.

In the other trench, there was what appeared to be a little stream, a man-made gulley of some kind. Your first thought was it could be somewhere to wash the mud from your ankles, but at the exact moment the thought entered your mind, you felt the Father's hand on your shoulder. You looked closer and saw the water was not fresh and flowing; instead it was still and somewhat lifeless. The shades of green and dots of yellow that you had thought were flowers and foliage now looked more likely to be weeds and moss.

You opened your mouth to ask a question and then closed it. For all you knew, you may have stumbled into them as you marched confidently away from your Father's house, completely oblivious to what you were walking through, your determination to follow your own plan carrying you through them.

He smiled. He knew you wanted to ask what these were but were feeling some embarrassment that you should already know.

'Trenches, that's what you're looking at. Two of them. Both very dangerous. They are the destroyers of churches and of families. So many of my lost children don't come home to me because they fall into one of these two trenches.'

There was nothing in His words that communicated fear or defeat. There was no intimidation or uncertainty in Him. But there was pain in His eyes. There was also an intensity directed at those ditches that honestly made you feel a little scared.

'I don't understand.'

'I know.' The intensity had gone the moment His face had turned towards you. 'Come. Let's talk as we go.'

Both of you walked on. A ditch either side of you. The straight level path in front, unremarkable in many ways, but solid and steady.

The trench on the left, the granite and stone – it's religion, the world of control and rules. You know it well. It's everything humans have done to make a system and a formula. It starts off with good intentions but then so often becomes a slow, painful death, a poison to joy and passion. So many first loves have died and decayed in that ditch. So many of my children, with so much potential to be history makers, nation-changers or family healers, have lost their way down there and lost the will to climb out.'

He stopped in His tracks and gently squeezed His hand on your shoulder.

'Do you understand?'

All you could manage was a simple and unconvincing, 'Yes.'

He smiled, a deep, warm smile for sure, but there was more to it than that; you just couldn't work out what, so you carried on walking down the road.

He went on: 'The trench on the right, the stagnant stream, well, that's the ditch of freedom. At least, it's what the people who go down there think is freedom. Only after it's too late do they realise they were never free for a minute down there. I know what you're thinking... all the worst sins happen down there, right? Well, yes and maybe. The brokenness that drives my children there, the seduction to self-medicate, to find an identity that is easy to accept and makes sense, the pleasure of the senses, all of it is down there. Pride is there too, but it's not as strong as in the other ditch. What sets this one apart is deep pain. So much pain is felt by those who choose to walk their journey down here. Hurting, broken children, all of them in pain and so scared to admit it.'

You had been listening, nodding, trying to agree with the tragedy of it all while simultaneously trying to silence every memory you had of time spent in those ditches; you knew you had made choices that led you into those trenches, even if you didn't know what they were at the time; you'd dwelt in them. Your mind was swimming with the memories but also with the only question you dared to muster.

'Father, how do you... how do we avoid falling in them?'

He smiled then and seemed to grow in front of you. Or maybe it was just the world around Him that was actually shrinking.

'You're doing it. Right now. The answer is right in front of you,' He replied, His voice echoing, rippling out of Him, even reverberating over your body and through you.

You kept walking down the middle of the road as a great light began to wash over the road in front of you. He filled your gaze and every shadow got pushed to the side.

When I started thinking about this subject and how it affects our sonship journeys, I was expecting to say something along the lines of:

- Making church structure or religion the focus of your faith = bad

- Using your freedom to do things your own way = bad

- Loving God and walking the balanced middle path = good

I think other books and teachers have probably made that point already. I don't think I need to convince anyone that the religious spirit and an immature use of freedom can be killers of the real joy-filled relationship with God we want to live. So this chapter isn't going to be about the trenches, saying, 'This one is bad and, oh, look, the other one is bad too!' We'll talk about both of them for sure, but we're going to primarily keep talking about the road we're walking and the One walking next to us on it. That's the real goal after all, right?

Walking the middle line can seem so *un-radical* for most of us. We have a propensity to lean in the direction of a life plan that will yield quick results, or at least, some immediate evidence that it is making an impact. The slower journey of trusting God for each day doesn't always come with breakthrough moments worthy of putting on social media. Yet no matter how many times we dress those options up as something new or different, they remain two perilous trenches.

One hard, with sharp edges and immovable stone steps, rigid and set in its ways. The other, false and alluring, beautiful from afar but stagnant and lifeless up close.

Too much control and too much freedom. The religious spirit and the spirit of the world. Doing it the way someone has told me I must, and doing it my own way.

These two trenches can only be experienced when we step off the road to the Father's house, or perhaps when we fall off it, or maybe get blown off it by a storm. We'll also find ourselves in one of these when we intentionally fling ourselves off the road. I don't think I'm the only one to have launched themselves into peril because I got arrogant, proud or just thought I'd spotted an easy way out of hard work.

Many of us have been in both trenches. We have even lived in both. We may have spent years in them. And we have probably made our way across the road from one trench to the other in an attempt to fix our lives from the problems caused by the previous trench.

These trenches are seductive and they present the greatest consistent temptation I have ever known, because ultimately they are about control. If I yield to the religious spirit I get the opportunity to put my trust in a system or set of rules, I can play the game and try to win by its rules. If I allow a false sense of freedom to draw me in, my focus becomes solely about getting what I want, when I want it, the way I want it. Both options stir in my heart the desire to either give up or to give in. They are both forms of control in an attempt to manage my life. What they offer doesn't satisfy, but they do go some way to temporarily numb the frustrations and the pains I'm harbouring.

So many Christians now live in these trenches. Some set up businesses or companies in them. Too many churches have been built in these trenches. Too many marriages started there or ended there. Too many friendships. Too many of us are conducting our relationship with God from them.

The road to the Father's house does indeed pass between both of these trenches, but it never leads into them, and staying on that centre line on the road, as it turns out, is much less complicated than we ever thought.

Less complicated doesn't necessarily mean 'easier', however.

Civil war

My wife, Abbi, and I once had a big argument about the Marvel film *Captain America: Civil War*.

It seems so silly even writing that sentence, but what started out as a discussion about the film ended up becoming a full-on moment of intense marital strife. The disagreement bore down to one simple point from the movie: one superhero (Captain America) wanted the freedom to be able to do his superhero work without checks and oversight, to go where he felt it was right and to use his power where he felt it would bring the most good. The other hero (Iron Man) wanted accountability, oversight, checks and balances. He wanted to do good but with a covering to protect them from inadvertently causing more damage than good.[45]

It's quite a political and moral conundrum for a superhero movie, and it was very interesting, but I'm not going to pretend that was my main reason for watching it. There's a giant battle at an airport and Spiderman shows up and things explode everywhere. I had to see it. Anyway, as far as our debate went, Abbi felt Captain America was right in his reasoning. I felt Iron Man was right. We went back and forth making our arguments, but after a while we realised we weren't really debating about superheroes; we were talking about the degree to which someone should be free and the degree to which they should be within a structure of accountability.

Freedom can be a gift… it can also be a poisoned chalice.

Structure and disciplines can save a life from destruction; they can also slowly choke that same life over years until there is nothing left. Both have the potential to bring life and both have the potential to destroy.

So, freedom or structure? Which one should we lean into? Which one is the safer one? Which one will help me grow? Which one does my church or my city, my family or my marriage need more of? Or less of?

I have spent much of my life pinballing between these two. Bouncing between being free and clamping down on that freedom – and all for the sake of my freedom. It hasn't often made logical or spiritual sense. To be honest, in my immaturity I have lurched from one to the other trying to find my breakthrough in a system or a quick fix, rather than finding it in God's Word and in my direct, intimate connection with Him. This chapter is about sticking by the Father's side in the midst of a lot of opportunities to try other options.

---

[45] *Captain America: Civil War*, Marvel Studios, distributed by Walt Disney Studios Motion Pictures, 2016.

The mosaic of the kingdom

I've been part of a number of different expressions of Church and religion over the years. I'm going to share a bit of my story – maybe you'll find some of yours in here too.

I grew up going to a primary school that was very high Anglican. Mass every week, Latin liturgy, incense and candles and statues of saints, it was all there. I sang in the choir and wore an important-looking cassock and silver-gold cowl. I was super-impressed with myself. Each service had lashings of ceremony and pomp, there were processions, the singing was all very formal and felt sacred, even if it was all in Latin and no one but the priest understood it.

Years before I experienced this, around the age of six, I was at the school's Christmas carol service. During the carol 'O Come, O Come, Emmanuel' I felt the Holy Spirit for the first time. I remember feeling very small in the presence of something that was very big but also very good. I didn't have language for it at the time, it was just a feeling in my gut in the midst of a very formal carol evensong, but looking back now I know it was the first time I felt the warmth of His touch on my life.

Around the age of fifteen, I joined a youth group based in a lovely village church. The church was very middle-of-the-road Church of England and I had 100 per cent joined because I'd heard there were girls in the youth group and no boys. I really don't think I was looking for God; I was looking for girls. It ended up being one of the most beautiful seasons in my life where I made friends, learned the value of the Church family and started my first steps into leadership. It wasn't too formal and wasn't too off the rails. It was safe and it was the first place I realised I was loved for who I was, outside my family. It was what I needed at that time in my life. I learned to feel the love of God through people and through little moments of His presence during worship. I wouldn't be where I am now without this church and the belief people there had in me, an enthusiastic kid who often spoke first and thought second. The church loved people well, and I was one of them.

In my student years and mid-twenties I was part of two different Vineyard churches in different parts of the country. I saw local communities being slowly transformed by practical love. For a few months, I sat in the passenger seat of a van that used to leave the church's garage every Saturday morning, full to the brim with furniture. We'd drive up to the house of someone in the community that had nothing and kit them out. As we heaved big sofas up staircases in blocks of council flats I started to see unchurched people experiencing Christians loving them well.

In my later twenties and thirties I entered charismania and all bets were off. I was hungry and desperate for a move of God, an encounter, a touch of His presence. I wanted to see the miracles of the book of Acts. I wanted to get free of wounds and pains from my past and I found that there were people who were freer than I was in God, and I was desperate for that. I joined a charismatic church called Catch The Fire, and it was like a second wind blasted in and out of me. I saw miracles on a weekly basis, healings that I couldn't explain away and moves of God so bizarre and unusual I felt I really was encountering the God of Psalm 115 who dwells in heaven and 'does all that he pleases' (v3).

The beautiful thing is that with each of these expressions of the body of Christ, I met, felt and touched the heart of God.

Each of them had its own philosophy and theology about freedom and structure. None of them was or is perfect. In many cases, too much freedom in one church led to people getting hurt and too much structure in another led to the Spirit being quenched.[46] There is no simple model of church where the balance is perfected. The many and varied expressions of Church around the world carry different aspects of God's character and focus. I believe we need to draw more from each

---

[46] 1 Thessalonians 5:19.

other's uniqueness rather than try to come up with a perfect model that pleases all. There is a mosaic of the kingdom across the globe of different expressions of God's people, formal and informal, loud and quiet, traditional and pioneering. It is part of His plan.

Jesus isn't against freedom or structure. He gave people a choice to follow Him and He regularly bent and broke the rules of nature to do miracles. He gave an invitation to all people, but also chose a key number of followers as part of an inner circle. He observed traditional festivals and He dressed in such a way that people recognised He was a rabbi and a teacher. He turned over the tables of the temple's money-changers, driving them out of the temple. Yet He also made it possible for Peter to pay the portion of temple tax required when it was needed so as not to cause offence.[47] Jesus cannot be put in a box. We have Christ in us and we are in Him,[48] so that means we shouldn't be in a box either.

God is the God of order and creativity. He is Lord of the cyclical seasons and the creator of wild flowers. He provides vivid colours and explosions of creativity and He makes sequence pattern and consistency. The magical flow of the aurora borealis comes from Him, as does the intricate design of a snowflake. He works in and through both expressions. In the mosaic of the kingdom of God, there is space for godly expressions of structure and freedom.

Have you considered where you naturally lean in these two areas? We all have a tendency to lean one way or the other, just like churches or organisations do. How do structure and freedom express themselves in your life? Do they lead to healthy things growing in your life? Do they lead to control or avoidance?

For many of us there can be a civil war going on inside us between the two. I'm betting that, like me, like each one of those

---

[47] Matthew 21:12-14; Matthew 17:24-27.
[48] Colossians 1:27; Colossians 3:3.

churches I mentioned, there are both godly and ungodly expressions of order and freedom in your life.

So what needs to stay and what needs to go?

Loving God is the main thing, right?

Here's a thought about 'love' that started to accompany my early days of stepping out of orphanness and into sonship. It goes something like this:

> I love God and I'm going to make the 'love relationship' the main thing. If I just love Him I will avoid persistent sin or selfish decisions. If I just keep this love thing going, then the temptations to control will pass me by and I will be safe.

It's a great thought, isn't it? Love God and let love be the thing that leads you. It is biblical. It's the first of the two greatest commandments, to love God above all other things.[49] It's the one thing Jesus is going to ask us about when we meet Him face to face, as I believe Matthew 22:36-40 makes very clear. This is a good thought.

Right?

Yes.

Phew. Did you think I was going to go controversial there? Breathe easy. Love *is* the goal. You and I living in a love relationship with God is the whole game. However, *how* we love God will be vital to our survival and growth and how much we are propelled or held back on our sonship journey. I'm a pastor at a 'love church', but I know that a love relationship alone will not keep our feet walking down the centre of the road to the Father's house. There is more to it than just intimacy.

When we focus solely on the love relationship between us and God, we open ourselves up to the potential of growing both

---

[49] Matthew 22:36-40.

cold and cynical about one particular posture before God that Scripture spends *huge* amounts of time talking about.

I'm talking about *the fear of the Lord*.

Talking about the fear of the Lord feels like an uncomfortable whiplash experience after all our talk about God's love and grace. However, it is something crucially important that we must discuss if we are going to talk about being sons and daughters of God.

Before we dive into the scriptural basis for the fear of the Lord, let me share an example that points to one of the reasons I believe it is so important for our safe next steps into sonship. Every time after I have sinned, willingly chosen to put my desires before God, I have questioned what led me to do it. Did I lose my love for Jesus? Did I go cold or lukewarm? What on earth happened that could have caused me, someone who loves God and the gospel, to allow myself to get sucked into a sin like that? The more I have dwelt on those questions, the more I have realised that though my love for God never faded, it could get crowded out or overshadowed by circumstances. The fear of the Lord is to be a foundational presence, rooting me and grounding me; it's meant to keep me fixed and secure, it's meant to sober me up and keep me reminded about who God really is.

As it turns out, the fear of the Lord is an integral part of our relationship with God. When we don't cultivate that posture of the heart, that protective shield it gives us is allowed to slowly erode to the point that if temptation comes knocking, we are vulnerable and exposed. If the most important thing in our lives is our intimacy with God, then the fences and walls that protect it are made of the fear of the Lord.

Jeremiah slammed the people of Judah in chapter 2 and verse 19 of his book, saying to them 'the fear of [the Lord] is not in you'. Their posture of awareness and humility before the God of the universe was gone. Without it they were not seeing the fullness of God. Their eyes had glazed over and they only saw what was in front of them, the bubble that they lived in, the bigness of human beings and circumstances and the problems they presented, rather than the bigness of God. As a result, the people began to abandon God and worship idols, and sought comfort from other places that could never satisfy. If the fear of the Lord is diluted, our ability to abuse our freedom sadly rises.

When the fear of the Lord is *all I have* and there is no space for love and intimacy, then I fall head first into that trench of religion. Everything becomes about keeping the rules, saying the right prayers – stand up, sit down, do the next thing on the list. Religion begins to rule and the heart is lost. Worship that is meant to bubble up from within in 'spirit and truth'[50] is long gone and faith slowly crumbles away.

However, *with only the love mindset* we are in danger of falling head first into a life where anything goes, as long as it can be considered 'love'. We lose the moral compass we need to survive and we start redefining what truth is because that's what everyone else in the trench of 'freedom' is doing. Truth becomes whatever we want it to be or need it to be. Throwing out or dumbing down the fear of the Lord in our theology allows space for our morality to be defined by culture and by our generation's loudest commentators.

The aspirational part of me knows that love should be all I need to focus on. The fallen, broken, potential grace abuser within me knows that without the fear of the Lord, I am in danger of going off the rails, not realising how far I've strayed until it's too late.

God is good.

God is also the one who makes the nations 'tremble'.[51]

I need to know Him as both.

---

[50] John 4:24.
[51] Isaiah 64:2.

So what is it... really?

> The friendship of the LORD is for those who fear
> him,
> and he makes known to them his covenant.
> (Psalm 25:14)

This is one of those verses that doesn't seem to make sense in the way we would like it to. The 'friendship' of the Lord *should be* for those who are nice to Him or say nice things about Him, right? Maybe those who tithe? It should be for the ones who soak in His presence or ask Him day and night for His will. The 'friendship' of the Lord should be for those who want to do life with God and live in obedience to Him.

Is it really for those who fear Him?

I'm exaggerating a bit here. Of course the 'friendship' of the Lord is for those who seek Him and choose Him daily. However, you can't argue with Scripture here. It says 'those who fear him'. That's not something you can paraphrase away with a different translation. It means the fear of the Lord.

So what is it?

We've talked about why it's important and why it needs to go hand in hand with the love relationship aspect, but how do we actually define it?

Is it respect? Is it reverence? Wonder?

Is it acknowledgement of the bigness of God?

Is it an inner purity in response to the holiness of God?

Is it actual fear?

Is it terror?

Is it fear of your life being blotted out of existence?

Is it to be scared that what happened to the Israelite who touched the ark or maybe what happened to Ananias and Sapphira might happen to you?[52]

---

[52] 2 Samuel 6:6-7; Acts 5:1-11.

Is it the childhood worry that Jesus is watching all you do when no one is looking?

Well, yes, kind of and maybe.

I am so thankful the fear of the Lord remains undefinable by a single word or phrase in many ways. That's the way it should be. It is beyond a simple paraphrase or simplification. It cannot be condensed. It is all of those things and no single one of them.

The fear of the Lord speaks to an acknowledgement that He breathes universes out of His mouth. It is the total awareness of the destructive power at His fingertips. It is the cowering before His total, undefiled holiness. It is reverence as one would have before a king but deeper and greater. It is the deep trembling awe that one has staring from atop a mountain or in the heart of a cathedral. It is the shaking of your bones when you watch your first thunderstorm and see lightning tearing across the sky and feel thunderclaps shaking the building.

It is all of them and no single one of them.

The power and majesty of God is held in Himself in perfect tension with the loving Father heart and personhood of Jesus and the Holy Spirit. Put simply, you can approach Him, touch Him and feel the tenderness of His affection… and you can also be planted on the floor hiding your face from the awesome power and glory that emanates from His being.

We looked at Psalm 34 earlier. Let's expand it a little and look at how it offers a beautiful biblical parallel in tension in three sequential verses of how God holds both these parts of Himself:

> The angel of the LORD encamps
> round those who fear him, and delivers them.
> (Psalm 34:7)

> Oh, taste and see that the LORD is good!
> Blessed is the man who takes refuge in him!
> (Psalm 34:8)

> Oh, fear the LORD, you his saints,
> for those who fear him have no lack!
> (Psalm 34:9)

David, who wrote the psalm, understands that the fear of the Lord brings blessing, deliverance and provision. Don't skim over that, for your life and mine, blessing, deliverance and provision can come through the fear of the Lord. That's pretty counter-intuitive for modern-day church language, right?

David wrote this thousands of years ago, though. This isn't new!

He, the one described as 'a man after [God's] own heart',[53] understood that you can 'taste and see that the LORD is good' – even as you fear Him.

We don't need to stumble off the path in the direction of legalism, or autocorrect and veer towards supposed freedom to find the right balance. When we walk alongside the Father as sons and daughters, we can love Him, be loved by Him and also fear Him, and that's OK.

It's biblical.

It's wise.

It's the way Jesus related to His Father.

It may well be the thing that saves us from falling into one of those two trenches.

The Mezzanine Floor

In Acts 9 we read of Saul the persecutor's first steps into his journey into Paul the apostle. It's an incredible part of the Bible, almost unbelievable were it not for the record of his life that follows. The murderer of Christians and most brutal tool in the enemy's hand was starting his journey to becoming the greatest advocate for Jesus Christ the planet has ever known. As we know from history, many churches actually grow under

---

[53] 1 Samuel 13:14.

persecution, and the early Church had experienced great persecution under Saul. With his conversion, however, they were now in a period of alleviation. For the time being, the persecution had stopped.

Acts 9:31 is an example of a church growing when it *wasn't* persecuted: 'So the church throughout all Judea and Galilee and Samaria had peace and was being built up. And walking in the fear of the Lord and in the comfort of the Holy Spirit, it multiplied.'

They grew. They multiplied. They had peace. They were built up. They did it all by remaining in the fear of the Lord *and* the comfort of the Holy Spirit.

The Acts Church, spread across many different regions and territories, had a game-changing understanding of God. They knew that the universe-creating God was holy, pure and utterly deserving of worship and the deepest kind of reverence and fear. At the same time they also had the beautiful revelation that He was the kind, loving and identity-giving *Abba* Father, who poured out His Spirit for all.

They had the fear and the taste.

They had the reverence and the intimacy.

They lived knowing the strength of God and the comfort of God.

They had the cross of Christ and the resurrection of Jesus.

They had that intentional space where both could exist.

The image I think of is a mezzanine floor. A mezzanine sits between the ground floor level and the ceiling of a building and holds a middle ground in a way that feels a little unnatural to the building's design, but works beautifully in creating more space and possibility where there was none before.

This early Acts Church sat on that mezzanine floor, perhaps built on the foundation of the fear of the Lord, while reaching up into the freshly poured-out comfort of God's Spirit. The fear of the Lord and the comfort of the Holy Spirit held in a kind of positive tension. Two arguably very different aspects of relating with God and experiencing Him, but also complementary and powerful when held together in tension.

The early Church operated in the revelation that the comforting love of God awakens hearts to the reality that He calls us 'son' and 'daughter' and that we have a place in His home. The Church also preached and modelled the fear of the Lord where we remember He is the Lion of Judah,[54] uncontainable, utterly pure and holy, leaving thunder and lightning in His wake.

To be a son or a daughter of God is to walk straight down the middle of the road with the Father intimately and powerfully by our side. It is to dwell on that mezzanine floor, where we are with God and fully bought in to both the fear and the comfort of Him. It is not a place of religious burden nor of abused freedom, but instead it is the safest place on earth to be.

---

[54] Revelation 5:5.

9
As Gold

It's early, much earlier than you're used to being up and awake, but today feels like a new day and a new you.

You're out of bed within a few minutes and changed into a nice woollen sweatshirt and jeans. A quick tug of the curtains and the haze of soft morning light and autumn colours floods into your room. It feels good. You feel clean, like you've had a shower, even though you haven't yet.

Opening the door, you see just on the floor, carefully placed, a hot, steaming mug of tea. Clearly He left it for you only a few moments ago. God, it seems, is always going to be one step ahead of you. You pick it up and take a sip. Just right.

It doesn't sound like there is any activity in the house, yet it feels like it's OK for you to just go about your morning. You grab your Bible and your journal and that nice weighted pen you found left for you on the table in your room, and you make your way downstairs. Crossing the hallway and passing the kitchen, you can see that something is already cooking on the stove in one corner and the slow cooker is bubbling in the other. Looks like something is being prepared. You leave it be and go and find your boots.

A few minutes later and you're outside in the fresh air. It's just warm enough to not need a coat.

And you stop and breathe.

So much has happened these last few days. Or has it been weeks? It's like a good kind of haze, being here in the Father's house. Days, months and years all seem to blend. You know there are times when you are out on that path and it can feel like you've not even made it here yet. Then there are days like today when you wake up and feel like you've never lived anywhere else. It doesn't really make sense; however, it doesn't need to, not this morning. You're here, you're still buzzing from the freeing love you felt wash over you. You know that the orphan who had the driving seat in your life is starting to vacate it, and the son, the daughter you know you are, is starting to slowly take their place.

You walk forward towards the little river and the small stone bridge. The water is trickling; it's a nice sound, the flow of the river. Putting your mug down on the stone bridge wall, you peer over. What is it about watching water that keeps you enthralled and at peace? It's the same when you sit and gaze at a fire, with its constant movement and change. Out of nowhere, you sneeze, and your arm bumps against the mug, slopping it over the stone and over your sleeve. So much for the perfect, idyllic morning.

Dabbing your top doesn't really work, so you just roll up your sleeves, and that's when you see them.

Scars.

They almost take you by surprise, like you'd forgotten they were there. Long, thin lines of red and pink, up your arms. They were the results and the effects of the parasite. The choice to allow its talons to dig into your arms. Talking to God about that parasite, not just one conversation, but many times of being honest and trusting Him with your worst... trusting His truth... has started to heal the pain that each one of these scars caused.

You hear a sound and turn to your left. Jesus is coming out of the side door of the kitchen. He's got a thermos mug with Him and He's smiling as He approaches. You smile back and subtly bring your sleeves down.

'Good morning.'

'Is it?' He replies.

You open your mouth and then close it, pondering how you should reply.

'How do we talk... I mean, I still can't get my head around how we do this... have a conversation when you know everything I'm going to say?'

He laughs and smiles.

Wow. His smile is something else.

'You've got no idea how many of My children have asked Me that. Focus less on the fact that I know what you're going to say and more on the fact that there's nothing you can say that will surprise Me or make Me pull back from you.'

You pause, take a deep breath and then speak. 'OK, so... You know what I was just doing?'

'Yes.'

'I mean... You know what I was just thinking?'

'Yes, I know.'

'So...'

'Child... those scars, I know their shape and depth better than you do, but here's the thing: what you're hiding from Me right now – if only you knew what a gift to the world they could be, you'd give them to Me willingly.'

You feel your face flushing with colour and heat.

'I can't show these to people, Jesus. I know we're working on the pain they caused and I want to be healed of that, I truly do, but I can't show them to others. I can show the little ones, maybe the scratches and the scrapes You healed. I'll show those and I know they will encourage people, but these ones... I just can't bring myself to tell someone how I got them. I know You don't condemn me for what I did, but I just can't trust that others will see me the same way when they see them.'

Slowly, Jesus takes your hand and puts His fingers on your sleeve.

'Can I?' *He asks.*

You've come too far not to trust Him now, and though it's not easy, you nod, and He lifts the material and reveals the cuts and the scars and the long, thin, red lines.

'What was this one?' He asks, as He points to one line running up your arm.

'Lord, You know what it was,' you whisper.

'I know, but tell Me,' He whispers back, looking into your welling-up eyes.

'That one was control – it was every time I hid from my own pain and tried to control my life.'

He glows. 'Watch this,' He says, smiling and looking down.

Out of nowhere a blinding white-gold light bursts out from the spot His finger was resting on. No sooner have you looked away to shield your eyes than it is over. You're not sure if it was hot or cold, or if it felt good, or if it hurt. Something went into you or landed on you, for sure. Looking down, it comes into sight; instead of the long line of a red wound tracing up your arm, there is a glowing, shimmering gold.

The scar has quite literally become a line of pure gold, fused into your arm, part of you.

'What the...?'

He laughs and puts His hand to your face, wiping away a tear, and then pulls you into a side hug, your arm still out in front of you both like some kind of masterful exhibition piece.

'This is my power, my glory, in your weakness,' He says, gripping you tightly. He turns to face you again, searching your eyes with His to see if you get it. 'This is the thing that makes it a gift to the whole world!'

You stare down at your arm, this thing you were hiding, ashamed of and hiding. Now that red, bloody wound, that scourge the enemy of your soul meant for destruction, was glowing back at you.

As gold.

'What does this mean?' you whisper.

I remember very clearly the day I heard someone tell me how they had tried to kill themselves.

This person talked of the isolation and the pain they'd felt for too long. They spoke about the stress of life, the false comforts and the sleepless nights. They had been struggling to find direction and they'd taken too many knocks along the way to cope with it all alone.

Scars, both literal and spiritual, were shown that day. I loved them for sharing and yet I felt utterly helpless to make things better in that moment.

But they didn't need my fix. They had revealed their scars and something profound was set in motion. They trusted me with the truth of what they had been bearing by themselves. Shame was lifted out of the equation. This was one of their first steps out of the prison they'd allowed themselves to be in. I believe it was of God. It was a turning point, as a red scar became a golden testimony in front of my eyes.

Nothing needs to be hidden any more

The first time I opened my mouth in front of more than a couple of people and said I struggled with pornography, I just wanted to die. How do you share testimony about something that you've felt so much shame about? How do you share about the very thing you've tried to keep hidden for so long? I think I probably stumbled through it, underplayed it, maybe attempted to be honest in part but also covered myself too.

Maybe, like me, you allowed something into your life that really sought to destroy you. It should never have been allowed near you, let alone been fed and nurtured, yet you let it in and you let its talons dig into your arm and draw blood. You fed it and treated it like it was doing you good. Like it was welcome. Like you could be a follower of Jesus and hang on to the thing too. It was really trying to destroy you. It wanted to wrench you from the arms of Jesus. As we've said, it was a parasite.

Two thousand years ago, Jesus did something on a cross outside Jerusalem that proved He was stronger than your wound, able to outlast it, out-think it, outplay it and outgun it. His victory was and is total. His ability to redeem things is incomparable, as we saw with the cross – something meant to bring terror and shame became the greatest symbol for hope the planet has ever known. I'm using past tense language here deliberately. On that tree is where it happened.

On that same tree is where your wound's redemption can happen.

Redemption thinking is kingdom thinking.

I believe redemption thinking is what starts happening in our mind when we start believing and trusting that Jesus is both big enough to win the victory and powerful enough to bring a transformation. This thinking allows something that was utterly hidden from God to become the most seen and perhaps the most beautiful part of His work in you.

In essence, what we allow Jesus to redeem ends up being part of the extension of His kingdom.

What we keep hidden and in the shadows remains unredeemed and still capable of great destruction. That is where the battle is fought, between the light and the dark. We want to live in a way that is open and in the light, communicating beautifully and authentically, yet the well-trained orphan mindset inside us nurses the parasite and rarely stays quiet:

> It's better for them if they don't know the full extent of my challenges.

> I don't want to freak my wife/husband out so I'll just summarise my struggle in the broadest terms.

> I'm a leader and leaders shouldn't struggle with this stuff. We should be above it or beyond it, or should have worked out how to deal with it by now. I need to keep this weakness, this sin, this scar locked down and out of sight.

> I'll go up for the repentance ministry but I'll be vague, or maybe I'll give them my 'number five' thing on the list... steer clear of the big ones.

If he/she/they knew how I'd got these scars, then everything I have could be at risk of being taken.

These are the thoughts of the spiritual orphan heart. They are the thoughts of someone one who is still letting fear interfere with trust. They are really rooted in pride, unbelief and shame. They are self-defeating and self-consuming. They are simply chains of a different kind. I don't say this to make you feel bad; we're just being honest about this way of thinking and not dressing it up as anything better than it is!

These thoughts sustain the open wound and give it no chance to heal.

They are not the thoughts of the Romans 12:2 renewed mind.

Throughout His ministry, Jesus repeatedly sought to connect with the truth of a person, not the mask or façade they were presenting. Whether it was Pharisees trying to trap Him, the woman at the well trying to navigate around her shame, or just simple, broken sinners seeking a healing miracle, Jesus wanted a real person in front of Him, not the mask, not the agenda, but the human heart that was willing to let Him in.

In the Gospels, when Jesus said He wanted us to 'believe',[55] we can understand that means 'trust'. He never turned away from a person who showed they were willing to trust Him. He still doesn't.

How much do we still invest in hiding our weaknesses and our scars from Jesus and others? Even after we have been pulled off the path of orphanness, and our restoration and rebuilding is underway in the side-by-side walk with God on the road to the Father's house, do we still hide?

Somewhere along the line, many of us in the Church started to believe that God wants us to be free of the chains that held us, but also wanted us to figure out all by ourselves how to attend to the bruises and cuts those chains caused. Paul

---

[55] For example, Matthew 9:28.

admonished the Galatians for thinking this way. We didn't get saved by grace, God's free favour, just to try to keep ourselves saved by our own fixes and control or good effort.

This simple agreement to focus less on fixing and more on living unhidden may take months and years to bear fruit in our lives. It all boils down to the same thing, though – do we trust God, as sons and daughters, that it's OK to share the real us with Him and others, or will we keep parts of us back and hidden, just to be safe?

Our wounds as gold

Years ago, the Holy Spirit showed me a picture of me binding up my wounds with terribly created home-made bandages. I was holding a wound on my arm close to my chest, cradling it and desperately trying to avoid looking at it. Then in the picture I saw God asking me to stretch out my arm and show Him the wound. I was feeling shame about the poor quality of my bandage, and also fear of seeing the blood and pus of the wound itself. The whole picture was pretty unpleasant, if I'm honest; the only thing that was good about it was that God Himself didn't seem repulsed by what He was seeing.

This picture highlights one of the problems we face as we come out of the spiritual orphan way of living and into sonship. We say we want to be healed, but then we fight the process because the reality of seeing our wounds becomes overwhelming.

In John 4, Jesus has a conversation with a Samaritan woman by the well at Sychar. This woman has had many partners, sexual relationships, and is an outcast from her own people. Jesus, filled with the Holy Spirit, knows full well her history and her cycle of repeated failure, but this doesn't stop Him from telling her that she has access to a gift that will transform her life for all eternity. Not only that, but He also reveals to her who He really is, the Messiah, something He has not done plainly with the religious leaders of the day.

One conversation with Jesus is enough to turn this woman's life around. She runs into the town and announces to all those who shunned her, rejected her and judged her for her sin, 'Look at my scars! This man knew them all and loved me still – come and meet Him for yourself!'[56]

And so they come and they meet Him for themselves; they have their own encounter with the Messiah and they believe. The whole town gets transformed. All because someone allowed Jesus and then others to see their scars.

There is something about the way Jesus' mercy, grace and compassion intertwine that when He gets near our scars something profound happens. It is like one touch from His finger suddenly makes them into something else entirely. Scripture tells us that His suffering was, in fact, our healing.[57] Jesus' wounds and ours meet, and in a moment something beautiful happens. Our wounds are fully healed, and not only that, they are turned to gold.

There is not an adult on planet Earth who does not have a wound somewhere in their heart.

I think many of us desire to be more whole and more free than we feel we are. We want that feeling of being restored, reset back to factory settings, wiped clean and made as new. Our loving God wants more than that for us, however. He wants us to see that there can be glory and grace where there was once only pain and shame. These scars have the potential to be symbols of hope for those who see them.

We no longer have to look at our feet, hiding our hurts, keeping silent lest we be asked about the things we still feel shame about. Slowly, probably with some false starts and some backtracking, we are being invited by Christ to look up at Him and look onward to where He is leading us. The direction He wants to take us may well involve others knowing what we have wanted to keep hidden for so long. The pay-off is the freedom

---

[56] See John 4:29.
[57] 1 Peter 2:24.

it will birth in the lives of those who are looking on, hungry and desperate for their own breakthrough.

Paul talked about glorying in his weaknesses as they were opportunities for Christ to demonstrate His power.[58] This may be a huge step for you, one you may not be ready to take yet. That's OK. I imagine it took Paul some time to get there too.

What hope could Jesus infuse someone in your world with, because they looked at your redeemed scars and wounds, saw the glint of gold and wondered, 'Maybe God can do that for me too'?

> By the grace of God I am what I am, and his grace toward me was not in vain.
> (1 Corinthians 15:10)

Only the nail holes remained...

In John 20:19-23 we have the recorded scene of Jesus appearing before the disciples after His death on the cross. They are hiding behind a locked door, terrified of being found by the authorities, and Jesus supernaturally appears in the room in front of them. The disciples recognise Him and know Him to be Jesus, which is an important detail because the Isaiah 52:14 says of His crucifixion that He was 'marred' beyond all human recognition. His whipping and scourging destroyed His body to such an extent that distinguishing Him as a human being was almost impossible.

Jesus, however, appears in front of them and they know it is Him.

He is their Jesus, as they remember Him.

Thomas, one of Jesus' disciples, wasn't present for this first encounter, but eight days later Jesus appears again to His disciples, this time with Thomas among them. Jesus, knowing what Thomas had said days before – 'Unless I see in his hands

---

[58] 2 Corinthians 12:9.

154

the mark of the nails, and place my finger into the mark of the nails, and place my hand into his side, I will never believe' – gives an invitation. He asks Thomas to put his fingers in the nail holes and his hand in the side wound.[59]

So the nail wounds and the spear hole remain.

But it appears that the signs of the scourging and the whipping are gone.

Have you thought about that before, why the holes in His hands and side remain, but the effects of that whipping and flagellation seem to be nowhere to be seen?

I spent some time asking God about this, and this is what I believe I heard back:

> The signs of the punishment for the world's sin, the whipping, are gone. The penalty taken and the record wiped away. The signs of the cross, the nail-scarred hands, the symbols of salvation, remain. They show that salvation is permanent and irreversible for the one who will put their trust in Jesus.

Jesus' scars were overtaken by His resurrection body.

However, the marks of eternal salvation remain.

The holes in Jesus' body are a sign to me that even though I am not there yet, He is eternally committed to me. My salvation is secured in Him. He will be the only One in heaven with scars on His body. *That is how deep His love for you and me runs.* As we said, the cross was plan A. God decided it was worth it to do this for us. Jesus will forever carry the signs of His love for us and the completeness of the cross in His wrists and side.

However, when I look at that image of the smooth, healthy, resurrected skin of my saviour, standing before His disciples, recognisable as the man He was, I can't help but stop and wonder. My 'fear of the Lord tank' just gets filled in that moment. I realise that everything I threw at Him with my sin and toxic life choices has been washed away forever. It is gone.

---

[59] John 20:24-29.

He doesn't carry it any more. No longer is He the scarred Jesus we see represented on the crucifix all bloodied and torn. In heaven He stands there renewed and whole.

And so too can you and I.

It's time to start allowing God to put His finger on those wounds. That thing you have been ashamed of, hiding or perhaps just trying to avoid, God wants to heal and turn into an instrument of glory. Jesus has shown in His own body that He understands the nature and importance of wounds. He has shown in His own body that all things can be redeemed; your wounds are not an exception.

10
Need, Want, Imagine

Are you living in the house, or are you slowly walking back to it?
   Yes.
   Both.
   Kind of.
   You're living there, truly. It's your home. It's where you belong now and it's where your stuff now lives. Your coat has a hook it regularly goes on. Your bedside table has an ever-so-slightly visible ring developing from where your most used tea mug has sat. Your Bible lies open in your room, because you know it's safe for it to be open where you last read, where you last scribbled your heart response to the words on God's heart.

   You're not an orphan struggling to find their way any more. Home has found you. It came for you.

   Your spirit got picked up, lifted high and put securely in the heavenly places of the Father's house the moment you decided not to turn and run away from His embrace but instead let it in. Something special happened in that moment and His home is now your home. You live there and you live from there.

   And 'there' has a lot of resources. A lot of faith. A lot of hope. A lot of perfect timing. A lot of just what you need when you need it most. And yes, it's got a lot of money too, though that's the least interesting thing it has. All of this is true and good and such a relief, because it means you don't need to stress any more. You can breathe out and lean back.

So your spirit, the part of you that has undergone a transformation, is waiting for the rest of you to catch up. Your body and your soul at this moment in time are going round the long way, walking on the road. It is hard enough to fathom how God is outside time and space, let alone compute how there is one part of you there at the finish line with Him and yet another part of you that is on this road with Him right here and right now. Yet here you are, side by side with God, your journey still unfolding, still happening, as the gritty, earthy, soul and physical part of you takes one step after the other.

There are two things going through your mind pretty regularly.

First, enjoy it.

Second, trust it's real.

You are walking with the creator of all things, the Lord all the universe, your father. He's literally right next to you. Enjoy it, soak it in, drink it up, absorb the goodness that is being with Him and around Him every second of this journey. Being next to Him floods you with everything Jesus said about Him; everything Jesus opened up for us to enjoy with the Father is glowing, reverberating and rippling around you, each step you take. The 'Christ in you'[60] is leaping as you walk with the Father. The Spirit swoops and soars in and around you, binding you to Him and then spinning you around and letting you glimpse something new.

There's not a single second with God in this walk that is like the one that came before it. What a thought. Enjoy it. Enjoy the journey.

But also… trust that it's real.

Trust that you are walking next to the One who has in His hand all the provision you will ever need. Every miracle you'll ever need is there. Every gift of healing is held in those nail-scarred palms. Every breakthrough, every miracle moment where you'll need everything to fall down in your favour is there. Every ounce of strong holding-love you will need when everything falls apart in your world is already being carried by the One walking next to you.

---

[60] Colossians 1:27.

You walk on and on, past fields and rivers. A path leading off to a town on your left. A cliff edge comes and goes on your right. Over hills and through rain and fog. Warm sunrises and chilly nights where sometimes the stars shine so brightly and other times you don't see a single one. You walk and you trust and you enjoy and you struggle.

You know as you go that you have so much need, for so many things. It would all be so overwhelming were you not walking with the One who is incapable of being exhausted by the needs of humankind.

So how do you approach this subject as a son, as a daughter?

How do you bring it up, the stuff that you need, or want, or think you need and want?

How do you ask and what do you ask for, and when do you ask for it?

'Child of mine… I really do love you. Do you want to talk about all these thoughts you're having, or would you rather just try to figure it all out yourself?'

'Provision' is a beautiful word. The Greek translations of the word from its biblical roots refer to the act of preparing for the coming days' needs, and the supplies set out in store for those taking a journey and so on. There is the name of God, Jehovah Jireh, the Lord provides and has already seen to the need. And then there is just the simple word in English that we have: provision.

Pro Vision.

God is pro vision.

I think I like this word now. I didn't used to; I associated it with fear and insecurity. The sonship journey God has brought me on has helped me grow in this area a lot. God is pro vision – He is for vision, for expansion. He's for you and me taking little steps forward to spread His kingdom. He cares and is mindful of what is needed to see the job done. God is for the things of His heart, even if they are a long time coming.

I taught a child years ago, when I was still a teacher, who was seeking to become a stage actor, singer and performer. When I first taught her at school she was six years old and was playing one of the sheep in the Christmas nativity play. After a few years, even though she was still young, she was spending regular evenings singing, dancing and acting as part of the chorus in a number of high-profile stage shows. She had gone from the nativity sheep to the West End in a few short years. Her journey had to start somewhere, though, and for her, the vision of being an actress started by kneeling at the front of a stage in a sheep costume while Mary and Joseph passed by on their way to the inn.

Many of the dreams and visions we have in our hearts come from God. I have found that either they seem to be woven into our very DNA, such that we just feel like we were born with them inside us, or they are dropped into us by heaven at some point in our lives. That coffee shop you've always dreamed of opening, or the house with the little garden at the back: they are from Him. The dream to run for office, or create a business that innovates in the most creative ways; that preaching dream you have to maybe one day share what God has put in you: they come from Him. The beautiful, overwhelmingly big and the little, seemingly small and personal are from Him.

Now, does *every* idea you and I have for our lives come from God? No, not everything; some things come from the soul and not our spirit. Other things feel so intensely like they are from Him and they never come to pass, and some of them feel alien and out of step with our life plan and then turn out to be from heaven.

Finding answers to the kinds of questions stirred up here is not easy or often quickly achieved, but when we nurture our ongoing relationship of intimacy with God, when we live from His Word and embed ourselves in community with others, we position ourselves to receive the answers.

The matter of provision is critical to those stepping out of orphanness and into sonship; it is not a subject to be feared. I say that because nothing used to scare me more than the thought of the money or the provision not coming through for me.

God is a resourcer by nature. It is one of the most consistent things He took the pleasure of doing throughout the Bible. He stopped the sun from moving for those that needed it. He made oven-fresh bread appear for a broken man and He put a tax-paying coin in a fish's mouth, as well detailed plans for temples and arks and travel itineraries in the heads of normal men and women who were just trying to work out what was next.[61]

He gives vision, He is for vision, and He equips the envisioned.

God is a provider by nature and by deed.

The problem with provision

I have not always thought of the whole area of provision with positive feelings. In fact, that is probably an understatement.

It was one of the hardest hurdles to clear as I started growing into my sonship. Time after time I got scared about where money and resources were going to come from. When a brown envelope came through the letterbox (almost always a bill!) I would find myself speaking in tongues[62] over the thing before I opened it. The worry within me would just rise up out of nowhere and deposit itself like a lead ingot right in my gut. I was great at preaching about God's provision; I was just rubbish at expecting it in my own life.

I would sing the songs about God being all-powerful, about how everything I needed was found in Him, and I could read the Bible verses and quote all the relevant passages and stuff that was meant to make me feel better and more secure about provision. And yet, fear would still grip me. Each time I approached my finances as an orphan, I felt the anxiety rise and

[61] Joshua 10:13; 1 Kings 19:6; Matthew 17:24-27; Genesis 6:14-16.
[62] Speaking in tongues, other languages, is a gift of the Holy Spirit. See 1 Corinthians 12–14.

the tension break out. It wasn't that I was meaning to approach the issue as a spiritual orphan – I didn't *enjoy* thinking about provision with anxiety in my heart – I just couldn't break out of thinking about it in that way. It was like wearing contact lenses with a filter without even realising it.

Fear and anxiety are often the first emotions people have when the issue of God's provision starts to become part of their sonship journey.

Along with fear of not getting what it needs, the orphan heart has to contend with a lack of expectation that good things are going to come its way. Opportunities present themselves, and instead of thinking, 'God could make a way for me to do that,' we think, 'Well, there's no way that's going to work.' Too many times I experienced this; rather than embracing a God-given opportunity I would try to talk myself out of it before I'd even considered praying about whether God wanted to see it happen.

I remember one time being offered at really short notice a chance to join a mission trip to Kenya for a fraction of the price it should have cost. This was going to be a trip of miracles and healings; we all knew it and could feel the anticipation. My first reaction to finding out I could get on the trip at the last minute was excitement and elation at the joyful unexpectedness of it all; pretty quickly, however, my well-trained responses to the question of provision started to kick in.

> I work two jobs. I'll never get the time off at short notice.
>
> How will I be able to afford it?
>
> There's so much to do in such a short period of time. It's a great idea but I think realistically it's not going to work.

The fact that God could part the seas and make a way where there was no way[63] was in my head, but not in my heart. It wasn't even close to being something I really believed in. The supernatural provision miracles I'd heard Him do for other people were just that – for other people. I allowed fear and scepticism to live in me and they left no place for a miracle to happen.

One further common element to the struggle came a few days later. Amazingly the time off work had been agreed and the door was open; now it was just the money issue. I didn't need thousands, but I needed hundreds, and this was in a season where I had given up full-time teaching to work for the church for free, so I wasn't rolling in it, to be honest.

I prayed a bit, I wrote some 'God, please help' prayers in my journal and basically crossed my fingers spiritually speaking and hoped something would fall out of the sky.

One day, in the church office, one of our senior pastors, Chlo Glassborow, asked how it all was going and if the miracle money had come yet. After I had told her that nothing had happened, she asked me what I had done to activate the blessing of God. Honestly, I'd done nothing. I hadn't done anything to exercise my faith in any meaningful way other than pray and keep it to myself. This was embarrassing enough, but then came the kicker: she asked if I had put my need online on Facebook.

No.

I hadn't.

I didn't do things like that.

I had been earning very well up until the previous year. I had my own place. And a nice car. I wasn't the kind of person to ask for money online. I didn't need people to know that this whole trusting in God and stepping into ministry thing wasn't going as smoothly as I'd made out it was.

I wanted people to know that I was living by faith; I just didn't want to do the 'by faith' bit.

---

[63] Exodus 14.

Honestly, I was hoping God would arrange for someone to just put a cheque in the mail in answer to my private prayer request. It's painful writing those lines, but God used the truth behind them to bring an important conviction. I needed to deal with another unfortunate aspect of my orphan-hearted response to provision. Namely my pride.

Now, pride can cause you to go one of two ways: to hide your need from people or to broadcast it constantly so that people feel guilted into helping you. In this case I was definitely doing the former of the two, but the orphan heart can go to either extreme very easily.

Many of us can be unwilling to ask for help because we don't want anyone to see that we have need. We don't want our friends to see us asking for money or resources. There were times when I felt like I was a hero, leaving my secular job, throwing in the money to go and chase calling. Then there were times when I felt like an idiot, watching my friends get married and buy houses and go higher in their jobs, while I tried to live on the kind of finances I had when I was a teenager. I did what so many of us do in this situation: I cared too much what other people thought of me. I also cared too much about my own reputation to the degree that I didn't want to take what I would have seen as a handout, even if the person giving it would have seen it as a blessing and a gift. The level of sonship I was exhibiting in this area was next to nothing.

So to sum up: I was scared of the demands of money, pessimistic of my chances of ever being blessed by God in the area of provision, and so full of pride masked as false humility that even if a blessing did come my way, I may well say no to it.

The kicker is, looking back now, it turns out my issues with provision weren't really about provision at all. They were about how I saw God and how I saw myself. I didn't trust Him for anything that was tangible or important. I wonder, with that attitude, how on earth it was that I trusted in Jesus for my salvation!

Approaching provision as a son or daughter

Ninety-eight per cent of the time, when fear is rising up inside us about something, the root of it will be that we are doubting the things God says about Himself, or the things He says about who we are.

We may be talking about provision in this chapter, but we're really just taking another swing at the orphan mind vs the renewed mind of a son or daughter. We've haven't moved on from trusting God. The orphan doubts the love of God when things come off the rails. The orphan loses confidence that the Spirit is still moving around them. They don't see the hands of Jesus around them when another clap of thunder joins the already brewing storm. The orphan's biggest problem with provision is trusting God. It's not being without stuff.

If 'God is love'[64] and He is Father, as well as Saviour and friend, while also being an attorney and a 'great high priest',[65] then His heart is well positioned to provide for us. Those things we need come out of His care for us, even more so than out of our desperation to receive them. The money. The spouse. The job. The exam results. The debt relief. The house. The healing. The breakthrough. The restoration. He is capable of providing, and as a Father who is good, He wants to be the one providing for His children. We cannot take away the element of mystery – God may not always answer our prayers the exact way we want Him to – but He does want to provide for us and He does know what we need.

So back to my story about the mission trip. Chlo wanted better for me than I seemed to believe I was worthy of. She loved me, but also wasn't pleased with my failure to ask God or others for the miracle provision to come. So, marching me into the office's prayer room with two staff members, she gave this charge: 'Pray and declare that this provision is going to come because your Daddy loves you. You need to believe it, honey.'

---

[64] 1 John 4:8.
[65] Hebrews 4:14.

And so that's what we did. Two willing colleagues and I prayed for maybe five minutes, made our declarations and then got on with our day. I then got on Facebook and put a post on about needing the finances to go on mission at what I felt was God's call.

Later that day I got a message from a friend from a former church. She and her husband had felt they needed to go through their attic and clear out a bunch of musical instruments that had been gathering dust and sell them at a garage sale. This was a few months before and it had come to a tidy figure, but they felt the money wasn't meant for them, so they hadn't done anything with it. Then they saw my post about needing funds for a mission trip and, without a second thought, gave me the entire sum. In one go my need was met.

Wait, what? It was that easy?

Praying. Trusting. Killing the pride and acting like a son who has a good Dad.

That's all it took.

Now, it doesn't always work out with that level of speed, but in this instance God came through and met my need so simply and without fanfare. He just met the need. In an instant the problem I had was no longer a problem.

I wish I could say that after this breakthrough moment I never struggled with anxiety about provision again. God moved me on from where I was to a newer level of trust with that one little moment, but sure, there are times when I still feel like a hot mess when a need arises. But after I settle down, I remember who I am. I remember whose I am. That then becomes the filter over how I see the situation. It changes my perspective.

Being a son means trusting that I can come to Him without fear, without pessimism or scepticism and without pride and false humility. Being a son means I know and believe He actually wants me to ask for exactly what I need and then trust Him with the rest.

It's biblical to ask God for what you need. Sons and daughters know they can do that. That's where we're going next.

Need/want/imagine

My wife and I attended a live podcast recording in London before Covid-19. It was for a podcast on the TV show *The West Wing*,[66] a favourite of mine. Twenty years on from airing, the show still has a massive following, and so Abbi and a friend and 3,000 others packed into the venue to watch three people on stage have a conversation into microphones. It doesn't sound like it should be fun, but it was great and we really enjoyed ourselves. The hosts, two former stars of the show and one professional podcaster and show fan, were talking in depth about the themes of the narratives, the greater subtext, the deeper meaning and life application of the story's lesson. It was funny and insightful, but the thing that stuck with me was that this was the first time in a while that I'd been somewhere public where I had listened to someone on stage talk about a topic in depth, and with a desire to find meaning and significance, that wasn't the Word of God.

I know that may sound horribly sheltered and like I live my life in a Christian bubble, which might be true, but let me try to explain what I mean. I listen to podcasts all the time, I play games, I watch the latest Star Wars or Marvel movie. I like being a nerd and finding out about the next big thing coming out. It's good switch-off time. However, it had been such a long time since I'd been in a room and listened to people talk and discuss how *meaning* was to be found in something man-made *as if* it were carrying the significance of what I see the Word of God carrying, but actually was just a TV show. It was almost like the show was their lens for understanding the world.

On the way home, my mind went to all the times I go into my Bible, how the Word of God truly is my lens for seeing the world, how no matter how many times I or someone pulled out some revelation from it, there would always be more to be found the next time. It is a well that never runs dry, a fountain

---

[66] *The West Wing* aired from 1999 to 2006 on Channel 4 in the UK.

that keeps bubbling over. It is the Word of God to us in all seasons, all trials, all circumstances, in lack and in plenty, in triumph and in disaster.

The Bible speaks very clearly to us about the providing nature of God towards His children. The ram in the thicket, the manna in the desert, the ravens carrying food for the prophet, the right wisdom at the right moment for kings and judges, the multiplied food and miraculously appearing fish.[67] These are just a few examples of times where God provided for individuals, crowds and nations when it was needed most.

The problem, I think, is that my humanity and yours takes a lifetime of walking back to the Father's house on that road side by side with God Himself for some of those most base fears to be addressed and healed. Our anxieties do not disappear on the day of our conversion. I wish they did, but it doesn't work that way. The areas in our hearts where we allow the most anxiety and fear to rise up are unfortunately also the areas in which we trust God the least that He is who He says He is.

This is helpful in one sense because it gives a clear signpost to where we need to go next in our healing journey. It can also feel unhelpful in the sense that it can be demoralising to look at the same issue time and time again. However, we have to remember that when it comes to provision, we are dealing with one of the most fundamental questions every human has to face: 'Am I going to be OK?'

Fortunately for us, the Word of God, the light in the darkness,[68] already had the answer laid out before any of us experienced our first need for a breakthrough. I want to draw your attention to just three portions of biblical truth that speak to God's heart towards His children, words that you can bet your life on.

---

[67] Genesis 22:13; Exodus 16; 1 Kings 17:4-6; 2 Kings 20:1-6; Judges 6:11-14; Matthew 14:13-21; Luke 5:1-7.
[68] Psalm 119:105.

Need

In Matthew 6 Jesus gives the disciples the Lord's Prayer. Just before He speaks those words we know so well, He gives this thought in verses 7 and 8: 'And when you pray, do not heap up empty phrases as the Gentiles do, for they think that they will be heard for their many words. Do not be like them, for your Father knows what you need before you ask him.'

Our Father knows what we *need* before we ask him. Shortly after, Jesus builds on this thought in verses 31-33 when He challenges them not to worry about what they shall eat or drink or wear, for 'your heavenly Father knows that you need them all. But seek first the kingdom of God and his righteousness, and all these things will be added to you.'

We're being told here that we don't have to flood the throne room of heaven with words, and we don't have to worry and be anxious about where the food is going to come from, or the roof over our head, because the Father knows we *need* these things.

The first principle of biblical provision is that the son and the daughter of God understand that their Father knows what they need. Their need isn't hidden. As legitimate adopted children, we can live with an assurance that He knows there are certain things we just need. It doesn't mean we live arrogantly or obnoxiously, but it does mean we wake up to the revelation that He has already laid out before us. He will provide for His own.

Need is covered for the son and the daughter. The spiritual orphan has to guess where it's going to come from; they have to strive to get what they can and hang on to it for dear life once they have something. The child walking back to the Father's house with God by their side learns a little more each day that they have that ring of sonship back on their finger and that this means their needs will always be met.

Want

When we skip ahead a chapter in Matthew's Gospel we see the issue of provision being addressed again. In verses 7 and 8 of chapter 7 Jesus says this to those listening, 'Ask, and it will be given to you; seek, and you will find; knock, and it will be opened to you. For everyone who asks receives, and the one who seeks finds, and to the one who knocks it will be opened.'

Chapter 6 was addressing need; here in chapter 7, Jesus is addressing *want*.

We are asked, requested and invited to bring our wants to God. The request comes in the midst of Jesus talking about judgement, bearing good fruit and caring for those in need. The context shouldn't be forgotten; we are being reminded that when we come to God with a desire for something we want, we have to examine how much we are allowing ourselves to be used to meet someone else's need.

Sometimes God's answer to someone else's prayer will come out of my wallet, just as many times God's answer to my desires will come out of someone else's.

Nevertheless, the inference here is simple but profound. *Tell Him what you want*. Exactly that. Knock on the door knowing what you want to ask Him about. Jesus Christ Himself is telling us that it is OK to come before the throne of God and ask for something we want.

Not only that, but Jesus goes on to say that He won't give a serpent when a fish is asked for (v10). He gives good things. He is incapable of giving bad things to those who ask for good. The son or daughter knows and believes this invitation. They know they can – Hebrews 4:16 says, 'Let us then with confidence draw near to the throne of grace, that we may receive mercy and find grace to help in time of need.'

Whether we want something physical, a resource or provision, or we just want to feel the touch of His compassionate love in our time of weakness, we are commanded to ask for it.

Ephesians 3 speaks beautifully of the love of God and the mystery of His grace. In it, buried just at the end after Paul has spoken about the length and breadth and depth of Christ's love for us, he offers this closing praise: 'Now to him who is able to do immeasurably more than all *we ask or imagine*, according to his power that is at work within us, to him be glory in the church and in Christ Jesus throughout all generations, for ever and ever! Amen'.[69]

The inference here is that we <u>need to do some asking</u> and some *imagining*. Part of God's glory is that whatever we can think of, He can think bigger. Whatever we can pray that might be good for us, for someone else or for the world, He can surpass that goodness and unfold something even better than our best prayer on our best day.

It gives God glory to exceed the imagination of humankind. It gives Him glory to go above and beyond. Our part is putting our faith in the majestic power and capabilities of God to do more than we ever could by ourselves.

I know that pride and selfishness can still be very present in our dreaming when we take those first few miles on the post-prodigal road. God loves us too much to give us everything we ask when we ask for it, because our imaginations are not yet fully sanctified. In other words, we can want stupid and unhelpful things for ourselves. He's a good Father and He knows better than to give us everything we can think of.

However, when in God's presence we wildly imagine and dream bigger than feels normal or comfortable, we are positioning ourselves as sons and daughters. Being around visionaries and dreamers is helpful for this, and it will expose really quickly how big you feel you are capable of dreaming, or maybe how much of a 'play it safe' realist you might actually be. Jesus gave the great commission in Matthew 28:18-20, asking us to go to all the nations and baptise all of them... He didn't invite

---

[69] vv20-21, NIV, emphasis mine.

us into the great compromise, a few nations, a bit of transformation here and there where we can swing it. Jesus had no problem dreaming big and expecting big from His Father. He also had no problem empowering some pretty ordinary people to step into that bigness.

The culture we have grown up in will have shaped how we see this issue of provision. You and I will need to look at our own personal history and examine where those issues of needs, wants and dreams have been either encouraged or shut down.

Did your parents or guardians manage their finances well? Was provision a source of stress in your household, growing up? What about the country or the culture you lived in, or the school you attended, or the street your friends lived on? Our experiences of provision will have been shaped greatly by our upbringing. Some people will have modelled well to you; many others will not.

Are there dreams and desires you have wanted to ask for, but haven't because of fear? What is in your heart to bring before God right now? What is holding you back? If we don't allow God into our past experiences of provision and what was passed down to us, we may find ourselves too scared to ask, too afraid to dream and too likely to go on worrying in secret about our needs. The world's wisdom will do its best to speak to all that, but it is only God's truth that can comprehensively answer and guide in the way we need. The truth is, He's aware, He knows and He wants to be involved.

Asking God questions

Having spent some time digging around my own life, I know now that my orphan fears, doubts about God's care for me, and pride can all derail the provision from heaven God wants me to receive. I also know that biblically God has asked me to rest easy in the knowledge that He knows what I need, He wants me to ask for what I want, and He wants to exceed even my best and biggest dreams. I get that I won't always receive exactly what I ask for, and I know that patience is a biblical value. Celebrating someone else's breakthrough can often be the catalyst to seeing the same thing happen in my own life.

In short, to think about this whole thing from a son's perspective is to know that there isn't a formula I can replicate to get what I need from God. Once again, I have to trust.

At the start of Luke's Gospel we have Mary and Zechariah both experiencing divine encounters with an angel promising some pretty miraculous provision. To Zechariah, it was a son born to his barren and elderly wife, a boy who would grow to become a prophet who would announce the coming of the Messiah Himself. To Mary, it was the miracle of becoming pregnant by the anointing of the Holy Spirit and carrying the Saviour of the world, the Messiah, within her. Both of them were, I think, overwhelmed by the experience. Both had almost the same response... *almost*. Zechariah asked for information on how it was all going to work out, information that he could put his trust in. Mary didn't doubt; she just wondered how this was going happen and exclaimed the truth that she was a virgin and this wasn't normal![70]

What is interesting in this example is that Mary was commended and got to hear one of the best promises of Scripture, that 'nothing will be impossible with God' (v37); Zechariah, on the other hand, had his mouth silenced (v20), which in my opinion was so that he couldn't bring any more doubt or limitation through his words and what was in his heart.

So what's the point?

Sometimes the difference between faith and doubt is so subtle we wouldn't even know it unless it was pointed out to us. Mary's trust in the Lord didn't stop her asking a 'How on earth is this going to work?' question. Zechariah's trust in the Lord wasn't at her level, and that's why his question had undertones of a need for reassurance in it. And this guy was the priest; he

---

[70] Luke 1:18; 34.

should have been way ahead of this teenage girl on the 'trust in God' spectrum. God continues, however, to look at the heart.

Mary had cultivated trust. Our cultivation of trust in God's words to us is what makes the difference between stopping short of faith because we need an explanation and taking a step of faith even while acknowledging we have no idea how it's going to work out. It may not seem like a lot, but a few words show the difference between Mary and Zechariah, and reveal a chasm of difference in their hearts towards God.

The questions we ask of God, the dialogue with Him in the 'secret place', reveal how far down the road to the Father's house we are. What we do and express in public is not the best measure for how we are doing. What happens between us and God behind closed doors is where the real evidence is found. These conversations and interactions with our Father and creator really will reveal how much we actually do consider that place, the Father's house, with all its resources, home or not.

Hear no shame in that, but do see it as a barometer for how you're doing.

As we slowly lean into sonship and away from spiritual orphanness, you know as well as I do that we get to situations where we don't know what to pray, what to do or how to be when things are out of our control. For all these times, we need friends and the family of God to carry us.

I needed a Chlo to metaphorically kick my butt into that prayer room to ask God for help. I needed a wife to look me in the eye and say, 'Write this book, don't worry about how we're going to get it out there or if any publisher will want it.' I needed someone to drop me a message on Facebook and say they had an answer to my prayer for provision.

None of us can do this on our own. No amount of anointing can make redundant the need for people in our lives. Sons and daughters need people. Orphans try to go it alone.

The kingdom of God grows and flows in moments when someone comes alongside you and reminds you that you are a son or daughter of God and He knows what you need, He wants to be asked and He wants you to imagine and dream big.

Trust He is for you. Trust He will provide for you. Trust a bit more today than you did yesterday. Get alongside people who will remind you of these things.

The issue of provision is one that quite simply will not leave us for the rest of our lives. It may not be money we are asking God for, but I bet it will be something else. A soul. A prodigal to return home. Government law to be changed. A church plant to be filled with people. A small group where people turn up and don't cancel at the last minute. A clear scan at the hospital. A child saying they trust Jesus for themselves. A car's petrol tank lasting just long enough to make it to the garage. You name it, we're never going to stop needing things.

This great Father released His Son, Jesus, from heaven to be the ultimate provision for us. Let us never forget that what we're asking for has already been released. Every breakthrough is found in Him. Every cash flow crisis finds its answer in Him. Every relational nightmare scenario untangles in Him. He is our need, our want and beyond our wildest dreams.

11
They Play

Your heart is full.

Or at least, it's on the way to being full.

Things are better. We can agree on that.

There's been something of a routine of late. You open your bedroom door; there's a hot, steaming mug of tea waiting on the floor just outside your room. You can't seem to beat God to the morning; He's always a step ahead.

You make your way through the house until you find Him. Sometimes it's the Father, and He's sat out on the porch, a book written by one of His kids in His hands. Sometimes it's Jesus, chopping wood outside the kitchen door for a fire later that night. Sometimes it's the Holy Spirit in whatever room you're in. Somehow you know He's there; even if you're not quite sure where, you know you're hanging out with Him.

Other times it feels like the house is empty, not as though God has gone, just that specific, knowable sense of His presence isn't quite there. So you walk on the road, and through the fields, and down by the river and into the town, and somewhere along the way you find Him or He finds you.

This morning when you open your bedroom door and find that hot, steaming mug waiting for you, there is a note next to it.

'Meet Me in the barn.'

The house has a big barn around the back. A large, worn wooden door is the only way into it and despite all the time you've spent in the grounds of the Father's house, you haven't yet made your way here. Curiously, there's no lock on the door, just a wooden bolt that can be opened from the outside.

You pull the door open and step inside. Straw under your feet and light streaming in through cracks in the wood. It feels like you've seen this scene before, maybe in a movie or something; maybe it was in a book that you read and you pictured it like this. You can't put your finger on it, but it all feels familiar and old and like some youthful part of you remembers it.

There's a tractor, and even though you're an adult you just have an overwhelming impulse to climb up and sit in the driver's seat. To the left, there's a pile of straw, looking like a cushion. Again your logical brain says there could be any number of tools or garden machinery underneath it, but you have this impulse to dive head first into it like it's a snow pile.

'Why am I looking at this like it's a playground?'

A voice speaks. 'Because it is.'

Closing your eyes, you settle yourself. This is one of those moments when He's here, but you're not going to see Him; you're just going to know He's present.

'It's time you remembered how much we used to do this together.'

Abbi asked me the other day what one of my first memories was. I knew the answer immediately as I'd thought about it before. My first memory is of being around two or three years old and being on my bedroom floor in front of my wardrobe, fixing it with my toy toolkit. As I was doing this I was explaining to God which bit I was fixing, in case He was unsure or needed some exposition. I don't know how long I was there doing it, or how much the little child version of me told God about what was going on, but it's funny and kind of sweet that my first memory is of playing in a way that allowed God to be part of it. I'm pleased that no one told me to do this; it was just natural.

I'm all for all the conversations about calling and destiny and activating our God-given identity for the glorification of His Son. If we're not careful, however, we could lose out on a beautiful value the Father has for us kids.

Play.

A lifeline... not an indulgence

Play doesn't really extend the kingdom.

It doesn't usually move us into the next level of heavenly calling.

It doesn't tend to be the primary way you would go about spreading the gospel.

It uses up time that could be spent on preaching to the lost or serving the poor or something.

It's not productive.

It doesn't really shape our mission, or help us strategise for the next step of advancement.

It sometimes requires effort and even sweat, so it can't be sold as always relaxing.

But God wants us to play.

Very much so. He is interested in us playing and He desires us to do what it takes to actually enjoy the life He has given us.

The Father wove play into us from our conception. It's not something you teach a child, nor impart; it's something each one of us comes with in our DNA code. So deep is it on the heart of God that it was even written into the animal kingdom. Dogs, cats, mountain goats, baby elephants all play. The desire to play is within all of us.

Now there are, of course, hundreds of books out there that will argue the scientific and psychological merits of play as a learning tool for children and adults. I'm not a scientist, nor a psychologist, so I won't step too heavily into that arena, but I was a school teacher and probably watched more play in my ten-year career than I did focused learning!

For children and adults, play can and does soothe and teach us. No parent sits their two-year-old down for a series of seminars on phonetic sounds and blends. They play, they read with them, they make weird faces, and cheer and laugh when their kid gets it vaguely right. Kids at school play. Teenagers play. Relationships are built on play. Success and joy and failure all unfold in the areas of play.

Without play, we as people would not have developed properly. We needed it.

Let me weave this into our narrative of growing in God. Sons and daughters of the living God who are led by the Spirit and want to change the nations for good *need to play*.

I've struggled with this one on and off at different times in my life. Sometimes I had too much play and I wasn't doing the work in front of me – just ask my parents how much they enjoyed parenting me between the ages of eight and sixteen. I have, however, experienced the other end of that spectrum; I suspect you have, too – the struggle to routinely make play a part of our lives. When my mental and physical health are not good, there is also a lack of good, life-giving play in my world.

'Yeah, yeah, yeah, I know this, endorphins and serotonin… taking time off, be healthy, all that, we all need it. I get it. Move on.'

That was my response for a long while when this topic was brought up – brushing it under the carpet, thinking I knew it all, nodding and affirming that I should be doing better. Nothing changed, though. I just felt a little guilty for an hour or so before I got over it and went back to my life as it was.

Play – good, life-giving rest – is important, and a casual agreement with the importance it has in our lives isn't good enough.

- Having no room for play in our life causes our sonship and daughterhood to become twisted and misshapen.

- Without play, we actually become worse at following God, enjoying God and being able to pursue His calling for our lives and the assignment He's given us.

- Play is meant to relieve stress, and when we don't relieve it, we allow it to build up.

- We start managing our stress in an effort to hold the cork in the bottle.

- We turn to false comforts to provide the endorphins and the high that play would give us.

- We laugh less and grimace or sigh more.

- We nip and tuck and try to make on-the-go adjustments so that we don't burn out.

- We put on a brave face and talk up how good God is, even though we're feeling like we're running on fumes.

- Joy becomes a theological concept rather than an experiential one.

Ultimately we wake up one day and find that we have wandered far from the Father's house, through the tall grass, and are now back on the dirt path of our orphan days. And we never saw it coming.

When good, godly play is absent, we suffer. When there is no place for it, our bodies take a hit. When play is sidelined, our emotions only have serious avenues to take; the road to delight is blocked off. When it's put off, replaced or shown the door, our minds fail to receive the renewal it can bring. When we dismiss play, we dismiss a part of the Father's joyful heart we could have had access to. When we reject it, we reject the Holy Spirit, who is the very essence of creativity and joy. When we say we are too busy for it, we make ourselves out to be busier than Jesus Christ of Nazareth during His ministry.

Why else would the children have come to gather round Him, if He wasn't fun to be around?[71]

Jesus 'came, enjoying life'

In Matthew 11, we encounter a familiar text. John the Baptist sends his disciples to Jesus to ask the one question that was more important than any other – is Jesus truly the Messiah (vv2-3)? In His answer, Jesus talks to the crowds around Him about who John really is and how their judgements are actually going to hinder them from growing. They see John as cutting himself off from the people and from feasting, and their conclusion is that he must be possessed by a demon (v18). Jesus is seen to be eating and drinking with Jews but also with Gentiles, sinners and undesirables, so by the same logic He must be worldly and not spiritual (v19). Jesus' conclusion is simple – judge what you see by its fruit!

The Phillips translation puts this little interaction beautifully: 'For John came in the strictest austerity and people say, "He's crazy!" Then the Son of Man came, enjoying life, and people say, "Look, a drunkard and a glutton – the bosom-friend of the tax collector and the sinner."'

Jesus 'came, enjoying life'.

I like that. Is it the direct translation of the Greek? Probably not.

Does it convey the character of the man Jesus as He lived on earth, turned water into wine at a wedding, spent time with His closest friends, ate and drank, brought joy to the needy wherever He went? Yes, I think it does.

I believe when we look at Jesus we see the 'fullness of God',[72] His complete character and the complete fulfilment of the Scriptures. To look at Jesus is to look at everything of God. If Jesus had a value for enjoying life, then so should we.

---

[71] Matthew 18:2-4.
[72] Colossians 1:19.

When the prodigal son returned home with his Father in Luke 15, the first thing to greet him was a party and a celebration. Food, wine, music, laughter, hugs, delight. When the father goes out to the older son, he invites him into that same celebration. When the shepherd retrieves his sheep, he calls together all he knows to rejoice. When the woman finds the missing coin, she too calls her friends together to celebrate and party. We're meant to enjoy life, feast and celebrate with others when the circumstances call for it. Work has its place and so also does play.

Does it mean we take the sin and the brokenness less seriously? Am I advocating that we turn a blind eye to the desperate needs of those around us, to spreading the gospel, so that we can all have a bit more of a laugh? Not exactly.

Sons and daughters of God know why play is important; they actually know that it is a lifeline rather than an indulgence. They know it can be the most beautiful point of connection with the Trinity and with others. Play, for the son or daughter of God, is simply allowing yourself to sit in a moment of joy and delight with God or with others. It may serve no purpose in productivity or advancement of your calling, but it can provide the rest and renewal that fuels your next day of pursuing your assignment. It can take the edge off stress and tension better than the false comfort of self-soothing behaviour can. The leaders I follow and admire, those who I believe are most in line with their identity in God, these people know that time can be made for play in the middle of the busiest season of their lives and that it might actually help them through that time, rather than distract them from it.

When you read the Gospel accounts, it seems the Pharisees were most vehemently against Jesus for doing miracles on the Sabbath. They knew the many, many passages of Old Testament scripture that left no doubt about how important keeping the Sabbath was to God. What they missed, however, was what the

Sabbath time was for. It was made for humans, not the other way around.[73] It was a gift from God to be enjoyed.

When we are stuck in the trench of a religiously constructed life, play can seem almost offensive as an activity. From that place it seems unproductive and frivolous. It becomes something for people who have got nothing better to do with their lives. When we're buried in the trench of supposed freedom, play can become solely about getting our needs met however we desire and at whatever cost. False comfort replaces the real comfort God offers and the nature of play gets twisted.

Jesus 'came, enjoying life'. He shared moments of joy with His friends and those around Him, and then He went on and performed miracles and turned people's lives around. The Son of God fell into neither trench. He walked the middle road and He showed us how to follow.

Play in the marketplace

In Zechariah 8, God talks about returning to Jerusalem and making the city once again a dwelling place for His presence. In verses 4 and 5 He says this through the prophet: 'Old men and old women shall again sit in the streets of Jerusalem, each with staff in hand because of great age. And the streets of the city shall be full of boys and girls playing in its streets.'

It's a simple but profound point: God's presence makes it safe to play and enjoy life. His presence brings the safety and the peace that causes all people, regardless of age, to do what is good for them, to be people of peace and delight. In these verses, it is the returning presence of God to Jerusalem that causes the children to play in the streets. Because He is there, they can play. That's a beautiful thought.

Now, this could be the fun chapter; the one where I say things like, 'Why don't you do something for you? What do you enjoy? What brings life to you that isn't work or ministry-

---

[73] Mark 2:27.

related?' I could say all that stuff and we could make some lists and some promises to do things differently from this moment onwards (don't get me wrong, I hope this chapter will stir some of those thoughts – ask the Holy Spirit to do that for you as you read on). Let me instead make a specific point about one of the values of play we haven't talked about yet, particularly for influencers and leaders. *Safety.*

Billy Graham regularly went fishing and played golf. Bill Johnson from Bethel goes hunting. Rick Warren, author of *The Purpose Driven Life*, collects bottles of hot sauces; apparently his collection spans more than 600 different kinds. My church's senior leaders, Stu and Chlo Glassborow, enjoy bird-watching and photography. My friend and colleague Tom collected a model race track from eBay and has race parties at his house with the guys.[74] As someone who looks to leaders above me, I can't tell you how safe it makes me feel, knowing that senior figures in the global body of Christ take time to do these things just for the sheer delight of them. I know there is a wholeness to their lives that doesn't revolve solely around the next ministry thing. Each in their own way has made a space allowance for the enjoyment of delight. The thousands of church members, the stadiums of people, the audience for the next book or message are not the sole focus in their lives.

Before the coronavirus pandemic, I started to go once a week to a club that met in an old Scouts' hall. They played board and tabletop games there and everyone who attended loved being immersed in story and adventure. I used to do these kinds of games when I was ten, collecting models and painting them, then one day as a teenager I just stopped. One day, God asked me why I had given it up. The best I could offer Him was that I had grown up and moved on to grown-up things. I can tell

74 billygraham.org/story/graham-family-trivia-what-fish-did-billy-graham-face-in-a-swimming-pool (accessed 10th September 2020), www.premierchristianity.com/Past-Issues/2015/January-2015/Profile-Bill-Johnson (accessed 23rd June 2020), Stuart and Chlo Glassborow, used with permission, Tom Allsop, used with permission.

you, walking into that club as a thirty-something man to play a board game with other adult men had me feeling a bit on edge; it was the first time in a long while I'd walked into a room full of people who weren't there because of a church thing. That was a wake-up call.

I was welcomed in, though – they were brilliant. I got a chicken burger with a hash brown and sat down to play a board game with some of the guys. We had a laugh, we nerded out for a few hours and then it all went back in the box and we went home. And I felt a little flicker of the Lord's delight inside me as I drove home; that it had made Him smile that I had given up an evening to go and play once again.

We don't grow out of a need for delight in our life.

It doesn't matter what our role is, where in the pursuit of our calling we are, how busy we've chosen to be or someone has made us to be. We need to play.

If we want to grow as influencers, as leaders, or grow into our calling, we will need this value. Having a meaningful place for play and for delight will make us safer and more enjoyable to be around. It will stop us from living life as if all depends on the success of our calling and assignment.

For me, an evening's play at a local hobby club added value to my life. It made my colleagues and friends smile, knowing that I went there. I think for those around me, it also allowed them to let a deep breath out as they knew that it was something for me that was not primarily ministry-based but was simply fun and put a smile on my face.

How would you describe the value of play in your life right now?

Every day, every week and every year

There is a prophet and itinerant speaker I know who has such a close and deeply profound relationship with God. The stories of God moving in her life are off the scale: encounters with angels, supernatural transportations across continents in the middle of the night, prophetic words given to her from God about people's lives whom she has never met that are so accurate they leave the person receiving them in awe of God. Despite all this, she consistently talks about fun and play. When she spent all night ministering to a church, even if it were one or two in the morning, she would make sure she and the church's hosts had snacks and nibbles and laughed together before everyone turned in.

She would pray, meditate on the word, sit in silence before Jesus…but she would also make time to laugh. I can't deny the fact that her closeness with God, the supernatural moves in her life and her value for play and delight all occupy the same space.

Now we don't all need to put down this book, start telling some jokes and then expect the angelic encounters to begin. The goal isn't copying what someone else does. I'm not a fisherman and I don't really fancy the whole model race track thing, so those aren't going to work for me. How you play, what you do – that's up to you, and you don't need me to suggest things you can do. But I will say this: I bet something you love to do is connected with something you either did or wanted to do as a child. Coming to the Father as a son or a daughter may well mean getting back in touch with the little version of you… not so you can find another thing to get healed of, but so you can find something that needs to be re-awoken.

I don't have the specific date for when I first became a Jesus follower, and though I have no proof and nothing but a simple memory, I think the moment I said 'yes' to God was when I was in that bedroom aged two or three years old, fixing my wardrobe with a toy screwdriver. I was playing and I was looking over my shoulder and up to the ceiling every few moments because I knew I wasn't alone. I knew He was watching. I had no theological language to offer Him, no prayer language or scriptures to pray from. I'm not sure if my mum or dad had explained God to me or prayed with me before bed; they may have done and I just don't remember. All I knew was I was in that room and so was He.

I didn't even know who *He* was. I just knew He was there. I liked that He was there. I felt rude not acknowledging Him, especially not explaining the game to Him. So somewhere in me I said 'yes' to Him and I told Him how I was fixing the wardrobe.

Far before religion told me to buck up and take things more seriously, to be productive and toe the line, the King of kings was crouching down next to me on my bedroom floor wanting to be part of my little game because it brought us both joy.

I believe it is God's heart for us to have a time of play every day, a full day of Sabbath rest every week and an extended stretch of days or weeks at least once a year where we can step away from busyness and let Him recharge our batteries. Something every day, every week and every year.

For our day-to-day needs, it has to be something good, maybe fun, peaceful or refreshing.

Every week we need to contend for our Sabbath. It doesn't need to be a Sunday or Saturday – the day of the week isn't the point; the day itself is. The value of that time is what you and I need to honour. We can't fudge on it, squash it with life admin or lethargy, and we don't want to cheat on it. Feast, rest, do a fun thing, get out of the house and be around people, or lock the doors and have just you time. Once a week, enjoy the day God set aside for you.

Lastly, yearly, without fail, step out of the flow of life and let the universe spin on without you micromanaging it for two weeks. Do whatever works for you. Go away with friends, have a staycation, switch off your phone, don't look at your emails, be as unreachable as you physically and responsibly can be. Be with God and take things easy. Pray and journal and *do you*, but be OK with the routine going out of the window for a while.

This kind of rest is not dependent on having the money to go and sit on a beach somewhere; it is about creating a space where you can allow things to slow down and for some recharging of your batteries to happen. One good, true week of that can set you up for months of work on your calling and assignment.

Daily.

Weekly.

Annually.

Rest and play.

Have the courage to know that not everything will get done, and maybe for some of you, be at peace with the fact that the world will probably carry on spinning if you take a weekend off. This is the part of sonship and daughterhood that isn't related to getting things done, or winning souls, or running to the next meeting. It's about our health.

I think a lot about that walk back to the Father's house, side by side with God Himself, God in three Persons. I wonder about the conversations about my sin and my mistakes, my hopes and my pains. I think about all the serious healing we will need to go through and all the walls He has to break down to get to the heart of what's really been going on inside me. More recently, though, I've started to think more about how He may want to ask me what brings me alive, what is it that He made that brings me joy, what would I like to do with Him once we're home?

I'm coming to realise that sons and daughters make space for this conversation; they don't run from it or try to divert God away from it because of some misplaced religious spirit. Maybe you should hold off reading the next chapter for today and spend some time with God and chat about how much delight and play is part of your life?

Sons and daughters play. They are nation-changers, history-makers and shifters of the supernatural realms over cultures, but they also make space for fun. And rest. And laughter.

They play.

Do you?

12
My Part in All This

You're sitting on the porch step of the Father's house, looking at the wheat and barley in the fields spread out before it, gently swaying in greens and yellows. You feel the warm sun-cooked wood of the porch step underneath you. Hope definitely seems to be in the atmosphere right now. There is a lightness to things inside you and around that you have not felt for some time.

It feels good, but also still a little fragile.

Your hand instinctively brushes your arm, along the golden line of healing. Your fingers brush against the other lines of scarring, the ones still in the process of being healed. It may well take some time. Your eyes look down past the woodland to the road leading to and from this place. You will walk along it again, many, many times more. You're not done yet.

You have hope now, though, and that changes things dramatically.

Hope has allowed space in you to be created for the one thing you actually needed to be activated: faith. Faith in Him. In one sense, hope was the lock and faith the key.

You reach down and pick something off the ground. It's small and brownish-green. It could be a seed or just some off-cast from a plant. It would be profound for this little moment if it were a seed; that would make this moment sitting on the porch of your Father's house even more transcendent and divinely inspired. Picking up a seed while thinking about hope and faith. You can't really tell, though; whatever it is, it's done the trick – it's reminded you of the verses... the 'mustard seed[75] *... the 'kernel of faith*[76] *... that thing that is birthed inside you that believes God can do something big... with your 'something little'.*

In all these months and years of struggling back and forth on the path and in the woods and trying to both walk that post-prodigal road and live from your Father's house, somewhere along the line, the hope you had for your dreams, His dreams in you and through you, fragile as they were, wasn't given the room and light they needed to grow.

Hope got deferred.

The tree of life wasn't able to grow.

The thing got rescheduled, put on hold, or just repurposed.

A lesser version of the dream became acceptable.

Whatever 'Plan C' was became the new focus and drive for your life. Anything better than that was just a pipe dream that was almost certainly not going to happen. Smaller miracles were asked for, which meant smaller prayers were OK.

Smaller prayers meant for smaller expectations and that meant smaller disappointments.

The kind of radical trust you'd always wanted in God was quietly asked to sit down and wait to be called upon sometime in the future.

Faith became a more conceptual, more theological notion in your mind. Faith that God would use you to be a world-changer or history-maker gently withdrew from the stage until it was off and out of sight.

'Small' became the best word to describe your vision, your belief in what God could do in you, and through you, and around you.

All these thoughts were swimming around your head so much that you didn't even notice you'd stood up and started walking. Almost catching yourself in the act, you realised you'd made it as far as the stream that runs by the Father's house and leads down to the lake. Still holding in your hand that little brownish-green piece of plant, you remember it takes something this size to see a mountain shift in the kingdom of God.

---

[75] Matthew 17:20.

[76] Matthew 17:20, *The Message.*

A collection of little canoes and river boats come into view, tied up to a post on the bank. They look seaworthy but like they haven't been used for a long while. They are just waiting there, dormant, almost. Made for skimming across the water gracefully, but right now just bobbing against each other, secured to the safety of the bank.

You look down the river that leads from the Father's house to the world beyond, every nation, every people group, every race... everything is out there. Lands full of people all trying to 'make it'. So many different attempts at what success should look like are held out there. So many seeking the platform, so many desiring a certain salary, searching out a life they were told they should have, or running from the life they've inherited.

You are a child of God now. You've always been, but now you know you are adopted as a child of the most amazing Dad. You have a room in the Father's mansion. You're His son, you're His daughter, and you know there is more. You know there is something better, you know it's available. And you, like Him, walk past those empty, unoccupied rooms in the Father's home longing for them to be filled with life.

So someone has to go.

Someone has to go to these nations and peoples and say something.

Someone has to dream for a song, or a book, or a business, or a family that is going to make a difference in one of those people's lives.

Someone needs to walk into the shops and the schools, to the streets and the towns and say, 'Jesus is Lord.' Someone out there needs someone who lives here to tell them that.

Someone needs to say there is still something worth hoping in.

Your issues aren't done with. Your brokenness still shows. Your wounds are not all turned to gold yet. And let's be blunt, you still do and say and think stupid, unhealthy and selfish things. But none of those is the last word on you any more. You have dwelt in His home. You have lived in the very room Jesus went to prepare for you in His Father's home. You have felt Him put His mark upon your life. You have His truth in your pocket and written on your heart. It may feel fragile but the hope within you is strong, it's sealed in blood, it can't be extracted.

You have a relationship with the living God, the Father, Son and Holy Spirit, and your trust in God is growing a little more every day.

And that makes you different.

In your eyes you may not feel it, look like it, sound like it or have the stories of someone who carries it… but you are. You always have been.

You hear His voice once again. You don't even jump or look around; you know there's nowhere you can go where He isn't already there and no thought you can think that He doesn't see. Is His voice audible or internal? It doesn't matter.

'So, what's your part in all this?'

In 2019 I was invited to Catch The Fire World Leaders Advance, a time where about a hundred of our global pastors and leaders gathered together to seek the Lord, cast vision and build relationship with each other. Just being there was a privilege, and for a week I was able to sit around tables with some of my heroes in the faith, worship side by side with them and watch and learn. We met in the Dominican Republic; it was a beautiful location, emerald-green seas as far as you could see. The only problem was, the heat was so oppressive. It was a muggy, humid heat and the hotel we were at seemed to have made the curious choice of not having air-conditioning in its restaurant area. This meant that every meal time I sweated through my clothing, and ended up having to retreat back to my room for an outfit change about three times a day. I hadn't brought enough clothes for this and so had to resort to using my shower as a makeshift washing machine.

At one of the first meals of the week I couldn't find a spare seat with anyone, so I sat down on my own at a fairly large table, grateful for an opportunity to sweat alone without bothering anyone, though also conscious I looked like Billy No-Mates on a table for twelve by myself. A few minutes later, one of the senior leaders came and sat with me, then another, then another. Quite by accident I seemed to have created the top table and was sharing my dinner with a collection of high-profile leaders, authors and megachurch pastors. One of them sat on my right. He and his wife pastored a huge church in South America. Every time he preached I just loved his energy for God, but also his authenticity; I'd not had the chance to tell him that yet. We got chatting and I complimented Him on his recent book. Conversation then turned to me. What was my calling? Who was I? What was my big dream? What had God put in me to change the world?

After a bit of false humility and fudging, for reasons unknown I eventually said that one of the things I was working on was this book, how it was about sonship, finding God enter your story and taking you the rest of the way. How it was about hope, regardless of how well you think you've done or are doing. I talked for maybe two minutes max.

After I'd finished He looked at me, with this big determined grin and a laugh in his words and said, 'Alistair, if you don't release this book there will be boats that never leave the harbour!' He then slapped me on the back, looked up at the ceiling proclaiming glory to God, and went back to his meal.

The Lord works in funny and unusual ways. This pastor didn't know I was a visual person, he didn't know that this image of boats not being able to leave the harbour was just what I needed to push me a little closer to seeing a dream happen. That's the dream of this book; that's what is in my heart. That boats would leave the harbour. That men and women who have given their lives to Jesus, and those who haven't yet, would know God is a good Father, that they are His sons and daughters, with all the rights and security that are due, and that they would know they are alive for 'such a time as this'.[77] That those who are stuck would find in Him the way to get out. That those who don't know who they are would discover it as they encounter whose they are.

I wrote this for people who look out beyond the harbour of their current safe place of security, longing to sail into the waters

---

[77] Esther 4:14.

and waves of the real sea beyond. I'm writing this because I'm one of them, just someone who is learning that beyond the harbour walls God can be trusted.

The journeys we dream of taking, the voyages in our hearts are important to Him. What you and I dream of doing with our lives matters, because God Himself has put so many of those dreams inside us. He wants all the boats to leave the harbour. He desires for us to put our trust in the great Navigator of life. It delights Him when we take a risk and believe He's got us.

Back to my story – a couple of days after this dinner encounter we were in a ministry time, bodies were everywhere, people encountering God's tangible presence, laughter, tears, all of it was happening all over the place. I was standing there taking it all in with my receiving hands out in front of me, and suddenly I felt a slap on my palms and a familiar voice asking the Lord to 'smash the champagne bottles'!

I'm not a seafaring guy, but I know enough to know that when you launch a vessel, you smash the bottle on the hull. You celebrate its launch and commemorate it as it crests the waves of its upcoming journey for the first time.

This is the heart of God, to celebrate the beginning of your journey and mine. He wants to get excited about the early beginning, the embryo. We think it's all about the end

Our cultural mindset is so conditioned to think about the finale, the success of our endeavours. Everything seems to build up to the exam results, the test scores or the project's completion. From my ministry position, it can be the number of people coming forward for prayer. For a musical artist, it's the amount of copies sold and the number of times something is streamed. For many, it's the pay rise and house upgrade. All of these are good and wonderful, but they aren't the only things God cares about, by a long shot.

God cares about the end and finishing well, that's a biblical principle; however, *God also cares passionately about the beginning.* He cares about the start. He cares about everything it takes to plunge into the cold waters for the first time and hold your breath to see if the thing will even float.

A scripture that every church planter, every entrepreneur, every person stepping out and trying something new should have written on the inside of their eyelids is Zechariah 4:10: 'Do not despise these small beginnings, for the LORD rejoices to see the work begin' (NLT).

You can't have 'small beginnings' without leaving the harbour. You will only ever watch others set their sails and slowly cruise beyond the harbour walls, then out of sight into the great unknown.

A song starts with a first line. A church plant starts with an idea in your head and then, sometime later, a living room and four people standing in a circle. A political run starts with a piece of paper filled in and handed in somewhere. A baby starts with a moment of conception.

What have the dreams in your heart been?

What would their 'small beginnings' look like?

Even if you have tried them before and they didn't work out, what would a new beginning for all your dreams look like as you come to God with them as a child, full of faith in your Dad? What if there is something pioneering inside you? What if there is something that could be so beautiful, it would cause others to launch their dreams too, simply because they looked at your life and the hand of God on you and believed it could happen for them?

God will speak in your head!

I love the places in the Bible when something desperately normal and completely supernatural happens at the same time. For example, when Jesus and the disciples are talking and Jesus asks them, 'Who do people say the Son of Man is?' They throw around a bunch of responses that other people give, and for the most part they dodge His question. Jesus presses them for an answer and Peter steps up and confesses, 'You are the Messiah, the Son of the living God'.[78]

Jesus loves the answer. He loves it because it's true, of course, but also because one of His guys just heard from His Father. He has been training these men for some time now, and here in this moment one of them has heard the Father's voice and has spoken out an amazing revelation as if it were the most normal thing in the world. Jesus tells Peter that 'flesh and blood' didn't reveal this to Him but it was His Father in heaven who gave this to him (v17).

What makes me smile is that Peter *didn't have a clue* where it came from. He just had a thought in his head and then said it. He had no idea the Father Himself spoke directly into his mind in that moment. He just said a thing and it turned out it was one of the greatest revelations ever uttered in human history.

I love stuff like that. God working through the ordinary to release the supernatural.

Peter was learning to be a son. He was learning to listen and trust that he'd heard right. He was learning it's OK to let out the sails and catch the wind a little. He was learning it's OK to answer a question directly to Jesus and not fudge or manoeuvre an answer that someone else may have already given. Peter was learning to walk in step with God.

We as preachers love to rib Peter for having a big mouth and just saying whatever came into his mind, no matter how dumb or awkward it was. We roll our eyes and make out that none of us would have had our feet in our mouths as often as he did. Let me offer this thought, though – this moment is the evidence that God was redeeming something that was known as a failing of Peter's into his most profound area of ministry.

God would use Peter this way and do it again, leading to the day of Pentecost when Peter would stand up and say the first

---

[78] Matthew 16:13-16, NIV.

thing that came into his mind. Three thousand people gave their lives to Jesus that day.[79]

Holding back may protect us from getting it wrong or the embarrassment of failing, but it also may stop us from starting to do something that God has put inside us. Something He may have whispered into our heads without us even realising.

Stones in the desert

Jacob had an interesting experience with a stone in a desert that can help us when we think about engaging with the dreams God has put in us, and what our part is in His great plan.

You probably know the story. Jacob is fleeing from the wrath of his brother and a whole host of family dysfunction, and winds up on the way to his uncle. He has to stay overnight in the desert and chooses to rest his head upon a stone, falling asleep. As he dreams, God opens up a vision of a ladder or steps to heaven with angels 'ascending and descending on it'.[80] He wakes up and utters a beautiful summary in Genesis 28:16: 'Surely the LORD is in this place, and I did not know it.'

It's not too dissimilar to the words uttered in a similarly remote place by the servant of his grandparents, Abraham and Sarah. Hagar, after she met God in the desert, rejected and alone, in Genesis 16, exclaims, 'Truly here I have seen him who looks after me' (v13), which in the Hebrew can be translated as, 'Would I have looked here for the one who sees me?'[81]

God gives dreams, encounters and touches of His presence to men and women who are broken, under resourced and desperate. It was the grace of a good Father that led to Jacob and Hagar experiencing heaven on earth in the way they did.

---

[79] Acts 2:41.

[80] Genesis 28:12.

[81] Genesis 13:13, ESV footnotes, biblegateway.com (accessed 8th April 2021).

Let's expand on this a little by going to the New Testament and some interesting words Jesus gives on the subject. At the start of John's Gospel, Jesus pulls the rug out from underneath a man named Nathanael and blindsides him with some prophetic revelation. He tells him that before they met for the first time, He saw Nathanael under the fig tree when he was all on his own. This blows Nathanael's mind.[82] Jesus responds interestingly, taking it a level deeper, saying in verse 51, 'Truly, truly, I say to you, you will see heaven opened, and the angels of God ascending and descending on the Son of Man.'

The biblical stories of Jacob would have been well known to Nathanael and the disciples. They knew all about the ladder from heaven, the staircase touching earth as the Lord's servants moved up and down doing His work, right in the place where this lone sojourner was.[83]

So what is Jesus saying here to Nathanael?

Is He reminding him of that story, and saying that He is that ladder?

Is Jesus evoking the imagery of Jacob's experience in the wilderness at his most desperate and lonely and saying, 'I'm coming to bring heaven to earth, just like Jacob saw'?

Is Jesus speaking literally and saying Nathanael is going to see the angelic realm and see Jesus as He truly is, unveiled in His full visibly glory? Jesus didn't refer to Scripture without it being deliberate. He didn't say things for impact alone. He said them for a reason.

In the Genesis story, Jacob falls asleep and dreams of heaven encountering earth, the angelic beings moving freely up and down this ladder. In John's Gospel, Jesus many years later says, 'That ladder is Me.'

Jacob just thought he was stopping for the night, resting his head upon a stone, for that was all that he had. He was on his

---

[82] John 1:48-49.
[83] Genesis 28:10-19.

own, in the wilds, and his personal circumstances were so dire that a stone was his pillow for the night.

Now, a few chapters earlier, Jacob had been given, even if it be by nefarious tactics, the blessing and the inheritance of Isaac. His older brother had traded away his birthright for a single meal in Genesis 25:31-34 and Jacob allowed a situation to unfold where he received the blessing that had been rejected by Esau, his brother in Genesis 27. He had been promised the 'dew of heaven and of the fatness of the earth' (v28), that the nations would 'bow down' before him and that he would experience blessing and favour throughout the world (v29).

Technically, Jacob should have been flying in his calling and reaping the fullness of his inheritance. Yet here he was, lying out in the wilds, no blanket and no pillow, head resting upon a stone.

That stone part really bothers me.

Wouldn't it be better to not put your head on anything than to put it on a stone? Why did he do that? Had he given up? Was it symbolic for him of how terrible everything had got and how far he had fallen from that hope and those dreams of being someone? Was it just a really comfy stone?

We don't know why he did this, though we do know that he slept and he dreamt and he saw the kingdom of heaven and unknowingly saw Jesus Christ and the angels. The promises of God were reaffirmed over his life and the inheritance of the blessing given to Abraham and Isaac was renewed over him.

Then he got up, picked up the stone that had been his pillow, poured anointing oil on it and, laying the *same stone* down, he called that place 'Bethel', which means 'The house of the Lord'.

With this act he dedicated his life to God and his story started to transition. The man who used to run from his problems started to learn how to look to God for help in facing them.

This was his turning point.

Because of this guy trusting in God, the people of Israel got their name and their national identity.

He took a stone that was associated with all his failure, all his lack and all his loneliness and it became the cornerstone of the house of God. It became the first brick in the building of something new. He anointed it, purified it, changed its nature from what it had been to what it was now going to be, and symbolically he laid it down as the first brick in the building of the house of the Lord on the land that was promised to him.

I'm sure you can see where we're going with this by now.

Jesus is the starting point. He's the bridge between heaven and earth. He's the One who can be in our midst and we may not even realise it until we wake up. He's the dream-giver. He's the circumstance-shifter. He's the One who can take a stone symbolising rejection and poverty and make it the foundation of a glorious, mighty new house.

You can be sleeping in the middle of nowhere with next to nothing to your name and still be in the right position for God to find you and commission you.

Just one thing

As we journey through this subject of dreams and visions, and our own personal part we play in God's kingdom, I think it is good to talk about the potential assumptions we could have. For example, many of us think we need to have a killer idea to be a dreamer or a visionary. We look at stuff others have done, how their gifting creates opportunities, or how circumstances open up, and think we'd better get on the bandwagon before it leaves. What I love about the stories we've looked at is that God seems so determined to use the broken pieces of His children's lives to birth substantially huge things. So we can ask, what's my stone? And what does it represent to me? These questions help us bring to God our humble hearts for Him to bless rather than our credentials and CVs.

We keep wanting to build on our strengths and expand what we've got, but God doesn't seem to be particularly interested in that method. Here are some examples of how I think God works:

- John was a talented man and ran businesses in the financial loan sector and debt management and yet lost it all, leaving him tens of thousands of pounds in debt. After being invited to church by a friend he gave his life to God and decided to put his skills to work for the kingdom. In the mid-1990s he had a desire to help fifty people in his home city of Bradford, England, and so set up Christians Against Poverty (CAP). By 2020 CAP had debt relief centres around the UK and offices internationally. The organisation has been applauded by many, from prime ministers to bishops, for its staggering impact on people's lives, bringing them out of debt and into safety. John Kirkby had a vision to help some people in his home town; what it really became was so much more.[84]

- In the 1990s, a group of five friends in Littlehampton on the English coast used to gather and play music together. They started leading worship for their church's youth group, but their influences were bands like U2 and so the usual acoustic guitar-playing Christian hymns weren't quite enough for them. They played rock but still kept it worship. Month on month crowds gathered, and the cutting-edge band started to get noticed. On the way back from a gig, Martin fell asleep at the wheel of his car not far from their house; they crashed and he had to be cut free. God asked him while he was in hospital what impact he wanted his life to make. He told God he wanted to impact the kingdom with new sounds and rhythms. Soon after, the band

---

[84] www.premierchristianradio.com/Shows/Saturday/The-Profile/Episodes/John-Kirkby-From-near-bankruptcy-to-founding-debt-advice-charity-Christians-Against-Poverty (accessed 1st December 2020).

Delirious? was formed. Their songs and musicality helped shape a generation of songwriters and worship leaders.[85]

- William suffered sexual abuse as a child at boarding school. It led to a life of brokenness and control, hiddenness and shame that he tried his hardest to get under control. A day came when his wife called him from his office to say she knew, and in that instant he knew what she was referring to. They met and he confessed the affair he had been partaking in and the brokenness he had been trying to control all those years. Eleven years passed where this couple sought healing, counselling and the help of ordinary people around them to keep them alive. As an intended gift for his kids, William wrote the *The Shack* (Hodder Windblown) as a way of expressing the pain and the healing journey he had walked with God. It ended up selling more than 20 million copies worldwide and helping those who read it experience the beautiful relational side of God as He comes alongside us in our deepest hurts.[86]

What do these stories tell us?

God wants to use the simple, the weak, the bruised and the broken. Those who will let God use the symbolic stone of their weakness as a cornerstone for Him to build with. They become God's chosen servants in the kingdom. Jesus, the cornerstone the builders rejected, is the proof of this.[87]

Every giant in the kingdom I have followed, every true hero in the faith, regardless of their ministry or focus, has had one thing in common.

Humility.

They have given God the glory.

---

[85] www.delirious.org.uk/document.php?id=1325 (accessed 14th February 2019).

[86] (accessed 2nd March 2020).

[87] Acts 4:11; 1 Peter 2:7.

It wasn't about them or their great idea. It wasn't about their name in lights, or their brand or following. It was about one name: Jesus. The humble King, the One who gave God the glory in all He did. He laid aside His desires and personal wants and needs and He changed the world.[88]

When we choose not to fight for our place in the world, when we have chosen to lay down the desire to be seen and known, and when we complement that with a determined and sacrificial fight to contend for that little flame of calling and vision God has given to us – then we will see the kingdom move through us.

As sons and daughters we are to follow this example. Fan the flame of the dream God put in us, let the desire to be seen and known die and be left behind on the path, and trust that His measure for success is very different from ours and that His starting point may well have more to do with our pain and brokenness than it does our gifting and successes. When we trust and do it with humility we get grace released to us, for God loves to give 'grace to the humble'.[89] That grace part is often the thing that makes the difference for a boat making it out on to those choppy seas in one piece.

Start dreaming again. Get those journals out. Find those prophetic words. Find the stones you used to rest your head on, and ask God what they could become.

Rey

A few years ago, the film *Star Wars: The Force Awakens*[90] came out and the internet melted down. Everyone on the nerdiest parts of the web was asking the question, 'Who is Rey?' As it turned out, Rey was the protagonist, the lead character in the

---

[88] Philippians 2:6-11.

[89] 1 Peter 5:5.

[90] *Star Wars: The Force Awakens*, Lucasfilm Ltd, Bad Robot Productions, distributed by Walt Disney Studios Motion Pictures, 2015.

newest Star Wars trilogy. Who she *really was*, though, was a big question in all three films. Was she secretly related to one of the lead characters from the earlier films? Was she a Skywalker, or something else? No one could answer for sure, and being a nerd myself I was fascinated just like all the others who were sharing their theories. I remember watching a trailer for one of the movies and, as it played out, her words echoed over scenes of intergalactic battles and great drama. She just wanted to know who she was and what part she was meant to play.

Despite the fact that in the story she had the power of 'the Force' and had gifting and abilities, and despite the fact that she now had influence on a galactic scale, she still didn't know what her part in the story of it all was. What she was able to do with all her power wasn't actually giving her the answers she needed. Her skills and abilities, important and useful as they were, could not provide an answer for who she was, nor what her destiny was meant to be. She had a question of identity.

A lot of people in and outside the Church find their identity in their gifting or their power. What they are good at, or what function they serve become the definer of who that person is. God gave you and me gifting and abilities, but they are not the source of our identity. Even if you're really, really good at something and everyone knows it, you are more than what you are skilled at. And if you are an all-rounder or you don't feel especially skilled at something, that doesn't inversely speak to your identity either.

In the Old Testament, David is held up as the standard in all possible ways one could be the standard. He's handsome, agile, charismatic, a leader and a fighter, a poet and a worshipper. He's a loving servant with a heart of honour, a wise king and a God-fearing man. The one thing that sets David so clearly apart from his predecessor Saul and so many of the kings after him is that David consistently seeks the Lord for what to do next.

Read 1 and 2 Samuel and 1 Chronicles. David is constantly asking the Lord what he should do. In 1 Samuel 19, David goes to the prophet Samuel for guidance, in chapter 22 he takes advice from the prophet Gad, and then later enquires of the Lord Himself, then again in chapter 23 several times... and again later in chapter 30... and then again in the second book of Samuel.

David asked God for wisdom... a lot.

David asked for God's next step every time it hung in the balance.

David sought the Lord over the biggest questions in his heart.

He knew what his place in God's narrative was because he was in constant communion with Him. He literally wouldn't make an advancement or a retreat without God's input. Now, what David didn't do was ask God if he should get out of bed every morning! When it came to his assignment and his calling, the role God had given him, he asked God constantly, and he never fell back on an assumption or an inference of what he should do based on his skills as a leader or his role as a king-in-waiting. He just kept on picking up the phone and calling God.

Let's just go back to Rey for a moment and tie this all together. The Latin and Spanish root translations of the name 'Rey', outside its Star Wars usage, speak of royalty, kingship and queenship. Sons and daughters of the Father, the Most High God and King of the universe have a sense of royalty to them, even if we don't know what it's meant to look like or feel it. We may not look like royalty, sound like it or dress like it, but we are royalty. Children of the King *are* royal children. Our gifting will be different, unique and diverse. Your gifting and skills may be widely seen by others and you may be a great influencer, for better or worse. You may feel like your abilities or talents are marginal and overshadowed by those around you. As the parable of the talents in Matthew 25:14-30 tells us, however, God is not focusing on the size of the talent we have been given to steward, but on the attitude of our heart towards it and our stewarding of it.

He has put dreams in your heart that will spread His kingdom around the world. Heaven could be populated because of your dream in God being realised. As children of God, you and I have access to the resources, the backing and the fathering we are going to need to see big God dreams come to pass.

We just need a little bit of faith to get us underway. That faith may need to be funnelled into believing that God's best for you is yet to come. It may need to be directed into a confidence that the one or two talents He's given could be used to create something really beautiful (and that you don't need to have five talents to be successful in God's eyes!). That faith may just need to plant itself inside you somewhere and remind you daily that you're a child of the King and that, like David, He just wants to be included in your steps into calling.

Here are some questions to consider. Invite the Holy Spirit to give you His thoughts:

- What did you dream about as a child or a teenager?

- Was there a dream that you tried to birth, only for it to be lost or put to one side?

- Is there something stopping you from 'leaving the harbour'?

- Right now, could you be missing how God is working around you or talking to you? Is He present without you even realising it?

- When you have been in God's presence and in close intimacy, is there something you have felt well up in your heart (a people, a nation, an injustice, or an idea) that is pure and not self-serving or about being known?

- Is there an injustice in the world somewhere that you just can't shake, and you know you're feeling the Father's heart for?

- Is there faith in you, as a child of God, to bring whatever is on your heart to God once again and see Him make a small beginning out of it?

13
Things Fall Apart

So it happened.

Things were going so well, you were flying, you were climbing up out of that orphan pit, you were really settling into your room in the Father's house... and the fear you didn't realise you still had suddenly surfaced.

'What if I'm doing well and then suddenly things fall apart?'

Seemingly a million miles away from the safety, the warmth and the glow of your Father's house and covering, you stand on a beach looking out at cold, grey waters.

How did you get here?

Weren't you just talking about dreams and visions and embarking into your future?

Where are the fields and the rivers, the trees and the road you were walking? Where is the light of the Son, the protective shadow cast by the Father? Where is the Spirit and the love you were resting in? Where is the house and where has the road gone?

We were just talking about your royal identity and the calling on your life, weren't we? The progress, the conversations with God, waking up and feeling like those decade-long struggles were finally being unworked and overcome. We were looking up and moving forward, free and full of hope and excitement... so where did it all go?

Something significant has happened, more than just a bad day or a tough week.

A failure.

A breaking.

A capitulation.

An attack.

A resurrection of the old you.

A resurfacing of an old foe.

A total and complete pulling-out of the rug underneath your feet at the moment you least expected it.

Things that were coming together and being connected now seem like they are falling apart, and you are standing on the edge of a storm looking out over those cold waters. An unsettling rhetorical question swirls around as the wind chills your cheek and yellow-brown foam washes up from the waves against your feet.

'Redeemed, free, restored sons and daughters don't experience failure in catastrophic proportions, do they?'

Somewhere, across the ocean before you, there is a voice, like a whisper carried across the waves. It's finding its way to you. It sounds like the Father's voice, but you can't hear what it is saying, even though you try hard to hear. You'd dare to believe there is something hopeful being carried in that voice but the waves are just so loud right now, and you're shivering…

You know He's there.

Somewhere.

But things have fallen apart and you need to know what to do.

In *Leading with a Limp*,[91] Dr Dan Allender talks about how we as Christians often like to do away with complexity and mystery and narrow down our theology to try to combat the confusion they create. We don't like situations that don't fit our theology; it doesn't matter what our denominational background is, we don't like it. When circumstances start off as promising and then go south, our belief structure is too easily thrown into confusion

---

[91] Dan Allender, *Leading With a Limp* (Colorado Springs, CO: Water-Brook Press, 2008).

because we never made an allowance for mystery in our relationship with God.

Sons and daughters of God cannot sidestep the mystery of the unexpected or the inexplicable. We can't do a journey in sonship and daughterhood and somehow avoid situations where everything suddenly implodes without warning. Let's talk about the story of Dunkirk to explain what I mean.

On 25th May 1940, the largest mass evacuation in history was hours away from beginning. Hundreds of thousands of British and French soldiers were trying to escape capture and annihilation by the German force in Europe. At this point in the historical narrative, we are well into the Nazi regime's expansion across Europe and they are riding a wave of unstoppable conquest. The main body of the British Army, the British Expeditionary Force (BEF), had been outmanoeuvred and overwhelmed in Belgium, and France and was in swift retreat. The BEF had arrived on the European mainland only a short while before, with all the swagger and hubris one would expect a leading nation to have. They had arrived on the continent expecting to deal with this German threat quickly and decisively. They were gravely wrong.

Their encounters with the advancing Nazi army left them beaten, routed, scared and defeated. The remaining forces managed to make it as far as the French coastline with what was left of the French defence standing bravely behind them to protect their retreat back across the Channel. But they were stuck. They couldn't get across. Alone, afraid and surrounded, soldiers waited on the shores of the beaches at Dunkirk, standing on the edge of the sea, desperate to get home. It was only twenty miles or so, but it might as well have been a thousand.

If you have seen the 2017 Christopher Nolan movie which shares the same name as that town,[92] you'll know something of

_____

[92] *Dunkirk*, Syncopy Inc, RatPac-Dune Entertainment, StudioCanal, distributed by Warner Bros Pictures, 2017.

the powerful sense of disconnection from home felt by those men. The sound of enemy dive bombers overhead, the U-boat-infested waters, the streets barricaded. Pressed in. Desperate.

I watched this film with my wife, Abbi, in the United States in a packed cinema in Minneapolis. I don't think it was actually a story many Americans were familiar with and so, as it unfolded, the tension and anxiety of the story had the three hundred cinemagoers enraptured. We watched the plight of those men, so cut off from their home, and it hit hard.

It got so under my skin that I had to excuse myself at the end of the film and go to the restroom to cry by myself for two minutes. That doesn't happen to me often, so why here?

I believe it was because *disconnection* is such a powerful feeling.

Being disconnected from people or loved ones is hard. The feelings of isolation Covid-19 caused to people of all ages and life stages across the world proved that starkly to us all. However, one of the worst kinds of disconnection I have ever felt is the feeling of being disconnected from God. There is an acute version of this felt by every son and daughter who knows the Father's house, knows the company of Jesus and the indwelling of the Holy Spirit, yet experiences moments when they can't see or feel God in the midst of darkness.

It is a feeling like I'm *here*… and He's… *there*. God is somewhere else, somewhere I'm not, somewhere I can't get to.

One moment in the film sums up what I'm talking about. Two naval officers are looking out beyond the waters. Hope is in scarce supply. It's cold, silent, overcast. The two men gaze out at the nothingness of the water before them. They know that *home* is so close, they can almost see it, almost touch it. It is so painfully close, but it is utterly out of reach for them and there's nothing they can do about it.

Isolation from home. It's the worst feeling in the world. Loneliness was, in fact, the first thing that God said was 'not good' in all creation in Genesis 2:18. Yet here, these men are isolated, completely unable to control or fix their situation, desperate to return to the safety and protective covering of their home, but with an ocean blocking their way.

I know part of the reason the tears came after watching this movie was because the World Wars and the sacrifices made by men and women younger than me, to give up their lives to fight for freedom and to stand up against evil, have always moved me. I know I was crying because I was identifying with that. I get that part. The part I wasn't expecting to stir me so greatly was seeing people who knew where their true home was and identified with it, but couldn't get to it.

These were not broken people who had messed up in life and were stumbling towards finding out who they were. These were people who had set out from home with an assignment, a goal and a calling and were trying to get it done. They had tried to do something good and right and it had failed.

Put it this way – they weren't prodigals stumbling on the path. To use our modern ministry language, they were people following calling. They knew what they wanted to do and they had set out to achieve it. Call it being British soldiers or belonging to a unit, they had a sense of identity and purpose. They had a home in Britain that was secure and good. Now something terrible had happened and they were out on their own, feeling isolated, cut off and under threat.

This, for me, is what makes the imagery so compelling.

Things had fallen apart for them and no one saw it coming.

Have you experienced something like this?

After the events of 2020 and the global pandemic, I think this is something we can all identify with.

Habakkuk

There is a prophet in the Bible called Habakkuk. His book is pretty short and we don't really know much at all about who he was, where he came from, or any salient details about his life. We simply know he spoke to God and what came out of him and through him made it into our Bibles. There is something we can discern about him, however, based on his name.

The choice of names in the Old Testament was important; they often communicated something about who the person was meant to be. The name 'Habakkuk' literally means to wrestle and to embrace.

This man of God, this conduit of the very words of God in my Bible and yours, was a man accustomed to wrestling with some things and embracing others. It may have been a name, but it was also a descriptor of the life he led as he leaned into God's truth and also contended with the circumstances he saw in front of him. The role of prophets in the Old Testament was to stand 'in the gap'[93] between the people and God. God's Spirit came upon them and they spoke His words for the people to hear and respond to; usually the message they'd deliver would be a call to return to God. This is what it looks like to be living 'in the gap' between heaven and earth.

Habakkuk has to contend with his fair share of strife and heartache. His nation is falling apart around him, hope is disappearing, the people are abandoning God and he, a lone, isolated prophet, is looking for some kind of answer or solution from God that something good is yet to come.

So he prays and he seeks God's voice, and the answer he gets to proclaim is that God's going to raise up the most godless idol-worshipping nation on the planet to be His instrument in dealing with Israel's faithlessness.[94] This is a million miles away from the kind of answer Habakkuk wanted, and he has to wrestle with the situation before him and the words that God's just given him. That's the recurrent theme of the whole book. Wrestling with the mystery of a situation that is just going from bad to worse.

Habakkuk, however, does something very significant right at the end of the book.

---

[93] Ezekiel 22:30, NIV.
[94] Habakkuk 1:1-11.

He embraces a truth.

At the culmination point of a seemingly hopeless situation, in the process of his wrestling, he embraces the truth that God tells him. He looks out into the grey, churning waters of hopelessness and he chooses to remain convinced that God is who He says He is and that He is capable of doing everything He has said He'll do.

His 'embrace' right at the end of the book is beautiful:

> Though the fig tree should not blossom,
> nor fruit be on the vines,
> the produce of the olive fail
> and the fields yield no food,
> the flock be cut off from the fold
> and there be no herd in the stalls,
> yet I will rejoice in the LORD;
> I will take joy in the God of my salvation.
> GOD, the Lord, is my strength;
> he makes my feet like the deer's;
> he makes me tread on my high places.
> (Habakkuk 3:17-19)

Habakkuk shows an amount of ownership here of his place in God's narrative. He is wrestling with what he can see circumstantially, and even the reality that things may be getting harder and more brutal, and rather than stepping back and aiming this word at the people of Israel, he chooses to answer it personally. He decides that he is going to choose to trust God, worship Him and endure through to the other side. He doesn't run and hide from what is happening, and it's clear he doesn't fully know what will happen, but he does decide what his posture is going to be regardless.

As a person living my life and as a pastor ministering in a church, one of the greatest challenges I repeatedly face is trying to make sense of life when things seem like they are falling apart:

- A miscarriage.

- A parasite of some kind finding its way back into a life.

- A betrayal.

- An opportunity turning into hell on earth.

- A promise broken.

- A dream utterly and completely failing.

- A church closing or a ministry folding.

- A marriage ending.

- All the progress in the world seemingly wrecked because of a wound that went untended.

- All the riches in the world blown and lost because of one moment of stupidity and selfishness.

- The sickness coming back.

- The prayer not working.

- The answer not coming.

Are any of these familiar to you? When things fall apart, many of us *endure* and wrestle. I don't believe God is calling his sons and daughters to simply endure and wrestle and try to plough through. I know that there is some part of that that is true. There are stages to coming out of heartache. There are times when we have to push forward and lean on faith in the invisible God. I want to add this conviction, however, that a son or a daughter who is led by His Spirit *wrestles* with the mysteries and realities of painful situations, as they also *embrace* the eternal truths of who God their Father is and who that makes them.

I am called by God to wrestle with what is before me as though my life depended on it, and to embrace the truth that my life really does depend on. And sometimes, yes, I am called to endure too.

God instructs us to be honest about the circumstances we're in. We're called to be authentic in the middle of the worst things we experience. Stepping into the reality of being a child of God and not an orphan means that we start to let ourselves be coached by the Father to embrace truth all the more in these moments than when everything is going well. The truth will transform us when we trust it, and our need to trust goes through the roof when things are falling apart around us. Believing that God is who He says He is in these moments of turbulence will do more for your soul and mine than it will at almost any other time in our lives.

Call it wrestling and embracing, call it something else, the naming of it isn't important. What is so crucial for a son or daughter of God, especially when everything that was good seems to have crumbled around us and isolation and fear start to rise, is to know this: our good Father wants the real us. He wants the stuff going on inside us to engage with all that is in Him.

What we feel, what we have experienced, what we have endured and what we cannot explain or rationalise – He wants it all given to Him. Entrusted to Him. Carried by Him.

God didn't get insecure when Job, David and the prophets asked Him bluntly what was happening in their lives, so it's OK to ask God what on earth is going on and cry for all of heaven to land in the middle of it.[95] God wants us, I'd even say *needs* us, His kids, to be honest about the mystery and the questions we have, just as much as He wants us to hang on hard to this truth – that home is still there, and it hasn't forgotten about us.

---

[95] Matthew 6:10.

Home came for you

> When 400,000 men couldn't get home, home came
> for them.[96]

That was the tag line for the trailer of the *Dunkirk* movie. I don't know if the movie studio or trailer creators or director knew how profoundly tied to the gospel this statement is!

When we couldn't get home, home came for us.

When we couldn't get to God, God came for us.

God had been in the business of rescuing humanity long before we placed our feet on this earth. A great unspoken misunderstanding of Christianity is that our salvation was the only time we needed rescuing. Don't get me wrong, whether you are saved or not is the most important truth about your life. But even saved people need rescuing sometimes.

I'm a pastor and a leader in my church and it turns out I need rescuing all the time. Most often from myself and the choices I've made, but also because I sometimes find myself in situations that have got out of my control. Now, I'm either more broken than most people, or most people are more broken than they want to admit.

Some of the soldiers in the movie *Dunkirk* try to deal with their brokenness and their situation with all kinds of terrible control-based decisions. Many overwhelm the first boat that arrives, throwing fellow soldiers out of the way to get a space. Others board vessels that seem like the salvation they need, not realising they are doomed to be sunk by the German U-boats prowling the waters. Some soldiers try to cross the Channel in tiny dinghies that have no chance of succeeding against the rough seas. One soldier is seen just wandering towards the

---

[96] www.youtube.com/watch?v=QdwVmHh1bz8, *Dunkirk*, Syncopy Inc, RatPac-Dune Entertainment, StudioCanal, distributed by Warner Bros Pictures, 2017, Trailer 2 (accessed 12th May 2019).

waters, slowly stripping off his uniform, removing hope as he steps into the cold water.

When things fall apart... we do this. We try to control or bring a fix. We try to rush a solution. We might try to lead heavily or put our faith in an attempted course of action that is doomed to fail. Perhaps, when things get really hard and we can't see a way out, we just give up entirely.

If none of those things sounds like you, that might be a good thing, but maybe when things fall apart you do what the rest of the soldiers did, the only thing they could do – wait and hope for something to change.

It is painful to watch the soldiers standing in lines leading up to the water's edge, all of them patiently waiting for a boat, a signal, something to happen. The only time they move is when they hear the scream of Stuka dive bombers as the next attack comes. They run and hide from the enemy as the bombs fall around them, tearing up the ground and killing their friends and squad mates. Then, after the attack ends, the men slowly rise from the sandy beach, dust themselves off and reform their queue in silence.

The disciples had an experience of everything falling apart when Jesus was crucified. Some just walked dejectedly home, heads bowed, mourning over a hope extinguished. Some ran and hid. They locked themselves away in fear and despair.

To each one of these, Jesus offered a rescuing hand.

To the ones who mourned on the road to Emmaus, He walked alongside and reignited their hopes. To the ones huddled in an upper room behind a locked door, He appeared supernaturally and left them in no doubt He was real. To the one who knew he had disowned Jesus, He gave the opportunity to redeem each one of those failures.[97]

Jesus is a rescuer when things fall apart.

---

[97] Luke 24:13-35; John 20:19-29; John 21.

He does not require me to regain control. He does not require my attempt at a fix. He does not need me to put my hope in a solution that doesn't involve Him.

Jesus asked those He healed questions: 'Do you want to be healed?', 'Do you believe that I am able to do this?'[98] It is my experience that He looks for intention and for partnership.

The men on that beach in *Dunkirk* got a solution they had been praying for in a form none of them expected when around 850 privately owned sailing ships, pleasure yachts and civilian boats crossed between 26th May and 4th June, saving more than 330,000 soldiers. No one saw it coming. Least of all the soldiers who needed rescuing.

All they needed to do was partner with the solution that *home* had provided, and get in the boats. They were expecting battleships – they got boats manned by civilians. Days before the evacuation, Britain had been called to a national day of prayer by the king. God's rescue to bring them home hurried on its way shortly after. When asking God for provision, we need to make sure we don't have idols about what God's answer should look like; we would do well not to have idols about what rescuing looks like either.

The river overrides the sea

When I first joined Catch The Fire church, I didn't really have any experience of the charismatic Christian movement. One of the terms that I struggled to get a clear definition of for almost two years was 'the river'. People spoke about it like we were all meant to know what it was, and, unhelpfully, I was pretty arrogant and full of pride about being a know-it-all in church things, so I did a lot of nodding and smiling whenever it was brought up, even though I didn't have a clue what it was.

After a while I learned to get some humility and I asked what this term meant. This is what I learned. The river is the flow of

---

[98] John 5:6; Matthew 9:28.

God's presence from the throne room of heaven. It's His intimate nearness as we experience it. It is the flow of His goodness and power from His very person. Ezekiel and John talk about it respectively in Ezekiel 47 and Revelation 22. This term is theological in a sense, but for me it's more about describing something I know I've felt, something I may have experienced and something I have seen and been part of. It's the landing, inhabiting and dwelling presence of God in a place where people are.

It is hard to describe, much like trying to describe water to someone who has not seen it or experienced the feel of it. I could tell them water is wet and free-flowing and warm or cold, refreshing or shocking, but to go into any detail I really have to use *water* to help me explain what water is. Now, I know a schoolchild could tell you the properties of water and the different forms it comes in, but to experience it is to understand it. To swim in it, be near it or drink of it will tell you what it is.

To revisit Psalm 34, we are commanded to 'taste and see that the LORD is good' (v8); that means we are to embrace what He offers so that we can see that it is good. Not the other way around. The river can only really be *experienced*. You can only get it by being in it, immersed in it. Theologically we can try to explain its properties, but it is in the experience of beholding it and being in it, as Ezekiel and John recount, that we will know what it is like to feel waves of the Father's love flow over us, washing us clean and restoring us.

We don't all need to have a full technicolour vision like these two prophets to have experienced it. We do need to taste it and see in our own way, though. We can do that by seeking it out, being hungry and desperate until we have found it. We can also experience it in the midst of a situation when we feel in a desert place and we're crying out for water.

Let me give a practical example of what I'm talking about. When Abbi and I got engaged it was just perfect – everything went right. I proposed on an island on Lake Ontario in Canada as the sun was setting, casting the city skyline dark against oranges and pinks. The photo I took on my phone was so good it is framed in our kitchen to this day.

At the time, Abbi lived in the States and I lived in the UK, and so after a wonderful week of being engaged, and a Holy Spirit conference thrown in alongside, we returned to our home nations. As the months went on, we realised that picking which country we were going to live in wasn't as easy as we had thought. Abbi was in a God-given position of influence in the Minnesota State Government as an elected representative; she was in her calling, in the middle of an assignment from God. I was associate pastor of my church in London, also doing what I saw as God's calling, in the middle of an assignment with doors opening up and growth opportunities all over the place. The more we talked, the more difficult it became to find an answer and the more obvious this ocean in between us started to become.

Up to this point, our long-distance romance had been just that, a romance. Every time we did a video call we were just getting to know one another; every visit to each other's country was a holiday. Now we were trying to organise a marriage, with a time difference and an impossible question. Who was going to give up their assignment from God to move?

We wrestled. We shed tears. We tried to convince each other without looking like we were trying to convince. We prayed. We poured our hearts out to friends and pastors. There was a point where we felt at such a dead end, the cold sea feeling so impassable, that I thought it just wasn't going to happen, that it was unsolvable.

I felt disconnected from God; people kept asking me what He was saying and I didn't have an answer for them. 'I can't hear anything other than my own stupid thoughts!' I'd want to say. I felt scared it was all going to crumble, and all my protective instincts wanted to kick in and make me run for the high ground, out of danger.

One day, during a trip to the States, I was trying to spend some time with God one morning and I got a ping on my phone. A friend had messaged me out of the blue to ask how I was feeling. It turns out this text was the thing that stopped me from making a drastic and bad decision.

I thought about it. 'How am I feeling?' Such a simple and obvious question.

I knew I was feeling anxious, overwrought, as well as scared and confused. But suddenly I was able to recognise that it was *my soul* that was feeling that. It was like I knew my skin was having a reaction, but under my skin all my organs and bones were just fine. Is that a weird analogy? What I'm trying to describe is that I suddenly realised what 'I' was feeling wasn't necessarily what *I* was feeling.

I knew that I was hearing God's voice speaking to me, but I knew it wasn't the only voice I was hearing. The voice of God within me spoke a little louder and said, 'You know how you're feeling right now… but you know that's not how you really feel, right?'

In the most undramatic way, I had a sudden revelation that the turmoil and turbulence, uncertainty and fear was all on the surface. Within me I had peace. I knew Abbi and I were meant to be together. I knew God was with us. I knew that any advice I had received or thoughts I had had in my head to step away from the relationship and choose an easier, more-hassle-free road were not God's thoughts towards me.

I tapped into the flow of intimacy within me. I stepped into the river.

The river I used to be so confused about actually started increasing its presence in my life. In a very non-dramatic way, it was like the waters of His presence had started bubbling up inside me, bringing hope and intimacy that hadn't previously been there in that measure.[99] The next three Sundays I was back at church, I poured my heart out to God and I wept. I knelt on that hard and dusty plastic floor in the school building our church rented, and allowed God to break me. I wept. I left

[99] John 7:38.

puddles of my own tears on that floor. It was uncomfortable, embarrassing and about as vulnerable as I have been publicly in my adult life.

As I pressed in, I realised just how many things there were in my life that I was unwilling to let go of. I was too scared to give up my role in the church. I'd worked for low money or for free for years and years, and now I was finally being paid and able to lead in ways I'd dreamt of. Selfishly, I didn't want to give it up. I liked being relied on by my leaders. I liked being their fix-it guy. I didn't want someone else to take my role. My pride was rampant.

The biggest fear I had, and I'm being honest here, was that I would leave our church and revival would break out the first weekend after I left. I had stupid pictures in my head of me being on the other side of the world watching it unfold on YouTube and feeling completely left out of it all. If I'm honest, my thoughts then started leading me to think that this would *absolutely happen*, and that my very presence in the church was the thing holding it back. It's crazy how easy it is to let your thoughts get out of control and start slapping you about.

I was being squeezed by the situation, and pride and control were seeping out of me in all directions. It was messy and completely unattractive.

But God used it.

He broke the fear of leaving off me. He got me to lay down a large portion of my selfishness so that I could look my fiancée in the eyes and say to her, 'I will happily and willingly move to be where you are if we decide together that that is God's best for us.'

As it turned out, Abbi had been on her own journey of intimacy with God. Revelation 22:2 talks about the river having trees planted at its banks and the leaves of those trees bringing healing to nations. Well, as I got a portion of healing for me, so she received a portion too. We decided, after all the praying and asking God and ourselves, that starting in London was the best choice for us. She came, got a job and in less than a year the

Lord had brought her into a role influencing Westminster and the UK Government for the kingdom of God. Beautiful.

The river, the intimate flow of God's presence, overwhelmed us both when the sea between us seemed impassable. The river surely did override the sea.

So what?

As a son and a daughter of God, we had a choice to either control and fix our way out of the turmoil we found ourselves in or to try something else, something more kingdom minded.[100] It seemed God's rescue plan involved both Abbi and me trusting Him to the degree that we had to take our hands off the steering wheel of our destiny and be prepared to give up all that we had worked for years to attain.

And yet He knew what He was doing. Even when things had fallen apart, He knew what He was doing. He wasn't far off. Indeed, His solution came from being within me – the 'Christ in [me], the hope of glory';[101] He just needed me to quiet down enough to hear Him.

This is my greatest encouragement to anyone reading this who is experiencing turmoil right now and is thinking of jacking in all this sonship and daughterhood stuff and returning to the old orphan ways.

Like those soldiers who could almost see the coast of England, their home, from where they stood on the beach in France, unaware that those yachts and sailing boats were speeding their way towards them, the Father's house is always much closer than we feel.

If you have experienced what it's like to grow in God and make progress, only to suddenly see it blow up in your face out of nowhere, this is a truth you need embedded deep in your heart. He's not gone far. Paul spoke to some Greek thinkers and

---

[100] Matthew 6:10.
[101] Colossians 1:27.

philosophers in Acts 17:27-28, saying that all whom God has made 'should seek God, in the hope that they might feel their way towards him and find him. Yet he is actually not far from each one of us, for "In him we live and move and have our being".'

When you are feeling the disconnection and the presence of those cold waters seemingly between you and God, when you are trying to wrestle and embrace, when you are trying to relocate the river of God's presence inside you, sometimes all He needs you to do is feel your way towards Him.

And find Him.

Even when things fall apart, He is not far from each of us.

> I will not leave you as orphans; I will come to you.
> (John 14:18)

14
Just the Heart

'Dad?'

'Yes?'

'I feel like I should be "done", we've covered so much and so many things have been opened up in me. I've seen miracles, I've been in the room when they've happened, and I've seen the kingdom of God flow into a situation and turn it all around. I've felt You, the weight of Your glory, rest on me, and I still don't have words to describe it. It's just… I still feel so unfinished, still so in need of help, still so in need of almost daily fixing or renewing.'

He looks at you.

Those eyes.

'Son, what's your question?'

'How am I meant to live, when I close my eyes and no longer see You and this house standing in front of me, when the world comes back into my gaze? The times when I get scared and tempted, or if I become a mess again? I need to know how to live when I'm trying to follow that calling and it's just so much bigger than anything I can do by myself… I need to know what to do!'

He smiles.

Oh, that smile.

Those eyes, brilliantly glistening in the light. No one in the world has eyes like that. They are flames of fire.

'Come on. Let's take a walk.'

You slide off the porch steps and take off briskly down the path.

Out of the grounds.

Onto the road.

Past the town.

Through the woodlands.

The river veering off to the west.

The signpost and the track to the far-off country goes eastward.

Then, not before too long, a dusty brown dirt path is beneath your feet. You remember it well. It's the place your redemption journey started. It's the exact place. The exact spot. The same pebbles, the same hedge, the same dip in the path. You stand there, this time with Him. His arm around you, staring at the spot where your journey back to the Father's house began.

'This is where your heart opened up to mine. This is where you let me in. And this is the place you must return to when everything falls down around you. This is where you and I will meet when you're ready. And this is where I will take you by the hand and walk with you back home.'

Your reply is weak even before it's left your lips.

'So there is no strategy to being a son?'

He smiles again and looks at you.

'You know I really do love you… so, follow Me.'

He turns and walks towards the setting sun, towards the house once again. Your heart is burning. There's nothing you want more than to be around Him, the One who has the answers, the One who has the presence and the hope that you need.

There are others on the path looking lost and desperate and in need of this Father. You beckon for them to follow too. All of you, hearts burning within, start to take one step after the other, following Him. All of you feeling the same thing, something burning inside.

Finally you get it; He just needs one thing from you.

If you haven't seen the TV show *The Chosen*, you just need to stop what you're doing and go and watch it.[102] At the time of writing, the second season is just beginning, with each episode depicting the life of Jesus and His disciples in the most intimate and human way I have ever seen, without losing an inch of the divine or supernatural. It's an anointed project, without a doubt.

Of the many beautiful depictions of Jesus interacting with people, the scene with the Samaritan woman stands out. We know the story, from John's Gospel, chapter 4. Jesus, sitting by a well, meets a Samaritan woman out in the hottest part of the day. She is rejected because of her brokenness and adulterous lifestyle, and yet accepted and known by the Messiah. *The Chosen* depicts the scene beautifully. They talk, back and forth, about worship and tradition and theology, but it's the moment that Jesus shows her that she is seen and known that she starts to understand. He looks at her and tells her that at the end of the day, the Father is simply looking for her heart.

That's all it comes down to. After all the questions, the analysing and the battle to understand. At the end it's about one thing. Just the heart. That is all God is truly seeking from you and me.

There are techniques and strategies and good disciplines that will help you to live more like a son or a daughter of God. I love them, I seek after them and turn them into reminders to ping up on my phone throughout the day in an attempt to embed them into my habits and mindset. That stuff is good and I intentionally pursue it, even when I know deep down that its ability to truly change me is actually very limited. What happens in my heart is what really changes me.

In the physical, the heart pumps life around my body. It keeps me alive and functioning. Without it, I'm a goner. In spiritual matters, my heart is the first domino. If a change can

---

[102] *The Chosen*, Season 1, Vidangel, 2017–2020, via free app 'The Chosen' available on IOS and Android.

happen there, it will make its way round my being and influence all of me.

We are very familiar with this process from the negative perspective. When we suffer emotional trauma, our heart gets wounded, and so creating or sustaining even basic levels of trust in people becomes hard work. We build a fortress around our thinking because we got hurt and are desperate to avoid it ever happening again. As a result we can spend a lifetime trying to numb those pains, hide from them or fake it before others that that we ever felt them. All just to protect ourselves. When Jesus touches our heart, wholeness seeps into all the dry cracks and sore wounds inside. Like honey or oil, it goes wherever it pleases, and parts of us get sorted out that we didn't even realise were dysfunctional or crying out in pain.

Our hearts are the entire ball game. A heart burning for Jesus will outlast a head that's been in churches for forty years hearing 'how to' sermons. I'm not against those at all, but the human heart needs more than that. Our hearts need to be captured by God's heart. He'll give us all the knowledge and wisdom we need, but He'll also set us alight for Him if we'll let Him.

My head and my thoughts will fall into line if my heart is right.

My soul will calm down and stop freaking out if my heart has Christ dwelling in it.

My body will be positioned for greater health and stability if my heart is not aching. In Psalm 51:16-17, David puts it this way:

> You do not delight in sacrifice, or I would bring it;
> you do not take pleasure in burnt offerings.
> My sacrifice, O God, is a broken spirit;
> a broken and contrite heart
> you, God, will not despise.
> (NIV)

Or as The Passion Translation paraphrases it:

For the source of your pleasure is not in my
performance
or the sacrifices I might offer to you.
The fountain of your pleasure is found
in the sacrifice of my shattered heart before you.
You will not despise my tenderness
as I bow down humbly at your feet.

Living this out day by day, with all the hidden fear and anger that we don't even know we're carrying, all our woundedness that will try so hard to drag us back to the orphan way, all that desperation to throw on a mask and fake it, will be addressed by this one thing... an undefended heart before Jesus.

In this last chapter I am not going to assume that you are 100 per cent secure in your identity as a son or a daughter now and that there is no trace of the orphan left. I am not going to assume that that you have a couple of nifty strategies here and there, and that you're now 'good to go' for a pain-free life of nothing but miracles and constant breakthroughs. So much of that will come for the son or daughter who believes, but that isn't what being a child of God is. It's not about strategies or techniques, it's just about the heart.

So let's keep it simple.

What matters most

Somewhere around 16th March 2020, much of the world changed unrecognisably.

Covid-19.

Suddenly everything stopped. The cars stopped, the streets went quiet, the skies became clear. The world was still spinning, but the activity all of a sudden just ceased for most of us. Things really did fall apart.

Even though huge global economic questions were being asked and the fate of nations hung in the balance, men and women, families and children, students and millennials, the elderly and the young were all asked to stay at home and self-isolate. Many were removed from vital support structures, asked to work alone at home, or to stop working entirely. For many, jobs and roles that gave value or purpose were suddenly compromised. In the space of a few short weeks, everyone's lives became much more simple. Much less polished. Much more vulnerable and I'd say far more authentic, for a time at least.

In the midst of this painful time, questions arose. Loved ones were suddenly in an 'at risk' category. Jobs that had seemed so solid and secure were now under threat. Ways of life so rooted and established were suddenly blown out of the water. I think two camps existed: fearing the virus or trusting God. Leaning into fear would lead to decisions being based on one kind of anxiety or another. Leaning into trusting God wouldn't necessarily eradicate fear or anxieties but it would stop them being the ultimate decision-making tools.

When life became so much simpler and more basic than anyone had ever expected, the issue of sonship, daughterhood and orphanness became hard to ignore for me. I knew once again that this wasn't a game of theological intrigue, I was going to either make daily decisions to respond to this global crisis as a son, or react to it as an orphan.

Whether we realised it or not, many of us started asking ourselves the question, 'What matters most?' When everything is working and the world is revolving the way it always has, we don't give an awful lot of time to asking questions like that out loud. Now that a pandemic was unfolding in every corner of the globe, we were forced to look at life differently than before.

About two weeks into the first lockdown, I started to get a sore throat. I had been on the phone most days the week before for about seven to eight hours, doing pastoral conversations and team meetings of one kind or another for the church, and hadn't been looking after my voice. Every time I swallowed, it felt like there was a cheese grater in my throat; it was agony. I started feeling down on power and my temperature started spiking. It wasn't until about two days into it that I actually considered it could be coronavirus. It just hadn't crossed my mind. But the more news coverage I watched, the more restrictions that were announced, the more prayer requests that came through, the harder it was for me to get my mind away from it.

Abbi and I had just moved into a new home about a week before the lockdown. In that first week, my uncle passed away and went to be with Jesus, not as a result of Covid-19 – however, because of it, there was no funeral or chance to gather as a family. A member of our church had a loved one go to be with Jesus shortly afterwards. Two weeks into living in this new place, in a time of great fear and growing evidence of the seriousness of this virus, and now I was sick. Then I turned on the news. A woman maybe five years older than me had died of Covid-19, after what she had thought was tonsillitis had suddenly got worse.

I don't think I lost my peace or my trust in Jesus at any point, but I do know that I thought about my life in a way I had never done before. What if my thirty-something years on this planet were all I was to have? What if this sickness was going to get worse? What if all those prophetic words and dreams were to remain unfulfilled? What would Abbi do? What could I say to her? What if by the end of this week I was going to be in heaven? All of this may have been verging on paranoid, but I can tell you I wasn't *asking* to have these thoughts. It was like they were letters being posted through my door; I was just receiving them and trying to tear them up. Despite how little I was desiring to have these thoughts, my mind kept going over them, and I asked the question, 'What matters most?'

In this book we have been constantly referring back to Luke 15 and the son's journey home. We have put ourselves in his shoes and started offering up our junk and our fears and all our attempts to fix things and make them right. And so, going back there one last time, we see and know that when the son 'came to his senses' (v17, NIV), he knew what mattered most.

Being in his father's house.

Under his roof.

Surrounded by his walls.

In his care.

Regardless of title, status, position or ranking, the son knew what mattered most was being back in the Father's house.

So the longer Covid-19 and the lockdown went on, and the more all the things I had relied upon were stripped away, I began to realise a little more each day how much I needed to be around Him, far more than I needed anything else. As much as I wanted solutions or strategies to navigate through this season, it was His presence, His company that was bringing me life. If the loss of shops or the ability to work with my colleagues was at one end of the scale, at the other was the real concern that I might be one of those statistics, one of those reported numbers on the news. Stepping back and looking at both the extreme and the trivial ends of the spectrum, I began to understand, just a little bit more, that He was my solution.

What I had with Him was what mattered most.

After all the words we have shared up to this point, it is the relationship that will endure long after the subject matter of dreams, resources or pain has faded. What you and I share with Him, that relationship, *is* what really matters most.

You only get ... to the degree you need to

My pastor Stu is one of the wisest people I have ever met. As a veterinary surgeon by training he thinks like a diagnostician, and so as a spiritual leader he thinks in a very spiritually diagnostic kind of way. Once we were talking about the concept of the inner healing journey, and specifically how it is we seem to revisit certain areas of healing that we thought we were done with. How is it that we can have an encounter with God, feel His touch in our lives, feel a part of our life changed... and then a year down the line seem to struggle with that same area again? Why did some of these pains, some of these struggles, come up again? Weren't they dealt with?

Stu turned to me and said these words: 'You only get healed up to the degree that you need to be.'[103]

This helped me hugely. It is a principle we must hold on to, and without it we could end up discounting hugely significant changes God has wrought in us, simply because we didn't realise that our need for restoration had multiple layers to it. When I look at the challenges I have faced, the fears and the self-limitations I put myself under, and then when I consider God's hand moving in those areas as I learned to be a son and trust Him, I need to remind myself I did get healing from those things, but I got as much healing as I needed *in that moment*.

Let me explain it this way. Imagine I hated heights and had stayed away from them my whole life, and then one day I get a job on the tenth floor of some new office block. I will need to deal with my fear of heights to be able to do the job. I will have to bring that fear to Jesus and ask Him where it came from. He can show me where it started, or how I first let it into my life, and then I can invite Him into those early painful memories and let Him do something about them. If I can trust Him with me, then He will enter that part of my life. He is a good God, He values me and wants me to be free, so in whatever way He chooses, He will come. I will feel His peace and presence enter me, and then I can take that peace all the way up to the tenth floor for my new job, and it feels brilliant.

I am healed. Hurray!

Then, one day, many months later, I get an invite to go meet the big boss up on floor twelve.

Wait – what?

I can't go up to floor twelve. I only got healed in my heart enough to make it as far as the tenth floor, and now I need to go higher! All of a sudden, my fears and concerns about heights come back and I start feeling like I did at the beginning, like I've made no progress at all. Shame returns, fear about who I am

---

[103] Stuart Glassborow. Used with permission.

crops up again, and all those feelings of strength I had as a son seem a million miles away from where I am.

Have you had some version of this? Why does it happen?

We get healed up to the degree that we need to be. God takes us a step at a time along the road, He doesn't make us complete the journey in one giant leap. You feel God minister in your heart where you got hurt in a relationship, but then when you enter into a deeper relationship with someone else, the old pains resurface. You allow God to provide for you when a bill comes up, and He does, but then six months later an even bigger bill turns up and you're spinning out of control. You forgive someone and let go of bitterness, but then the same person does something else and your heart is hurting all over again.

Jonah experienced this. In the book of his name, we read that his fear and his judgements led him to run away from God, and to him spending three days inside a fish to think over his life. From this place he entered a beautiful moment of humility, realised the goodness of God and got his heart right. The Lord released him from the fish's belly, he was now ready to do the work he was asked to do with the right heart, and so he did. An entire city was saved. Only a short while later, however, after seeing the mercy of God at work, no less, Jonah went right back into his judgements and anger. The same issues that caused him to run and hide before were seemingly back, causing him to want to curl up and die! The Lord had to talk to Jonah about His mercy and kindness and go another layer deeper on the same presenting issue inside him.

God is far more interested in maturing us than fixing us.

We can't grow into the person He made us to be if He takes away all our problems the moment they arise. I know this may sound obvious and basic, but it is a core growth component for adopted children of God. We miss it so often because we think when we get healed or free of something that *this will be the last time we have to deal with that issue*. The Father leads us on the road of sonship one step at a time, one need addressed at a time, and so we only mature to the degree that we need to be at that stage in our life. We get healed to the degree we need to be. And we often only develop intimacy with God to the degree we feel we need it.

We shouldn't feel bad about it being a process and taking time. Any parent knows their child will gradually start becoming more independent, more confident and more experienced the more they grow. With the kids I taught in those classrooms all those years ago, sometimes I'd have to revisit yesterday's lesson before starting that day's new topic. That was OK, though, it was school, it was the way it was meant to work. The sonship journey is step by step. As we mature, it is most often our needs that bring us back to God. He doesn't mind this as He is patient enough to wait for us to look up from His hand to His face.

Hunger and desperation

I see three general areas of need in our lives:

- First the critical needs. I need air to breathe, I need water in my body, I need food in my belly. These are things I need to function, to be alive and to live out my life. We've covered this already – Matthew 6 – God knows we need these things to live.

- Another level of need looks like this – I get into trouble sometimes and I need to get out of it. Problems appear and I need solutions. Need here is arising because of my circumstances.

- A third type of need is this – that there are things that are so important I recognise that I need them, even if I don't have them and even if technically I could live without them. I need love, I need purpose, I need intimacy, I need to know and be known by my creator.

The first level of need will drive us to God; it will cause us to cry out to Him. I remember driving to work one day and all of a sudden a car spun out in front of me and almost took me off the road. The first word out of my mouth with less than a split second's thought was 'Jesus!', not as an exclamation or swear word, but a cry to Him for help. It was actually a hugely encouraging moment for me to know that His name was the first thing I'd cry when I needed rescuing, and rescue me He did! Our need for survival and safety can bring us to God. He will always respond to that cry. He is a saviour by nature.

The second level of need is the one where God seems to do the most discipling and maturing in our hearts by using and redeeming circumstances to bring out more sonship and daughterhood in us. He will use those times to mature us, to give us opportunities to trust that He will provide, to trust that He will really use us, or to learn to trust that others can be safe. It can feel painfully slow sometimes, but there is a reason God used Abraham, Moses, Jacob and David after long stints in the desert, shepherding. We mature over years of small moments of trusting God with our needs. Our faith increases for finances or miracles the more times we trust Him to provide and to act sovereignly. In short, we have to see some stuff and go through some stuff, holding God's hand until we come out the other end, to grow as sons and daughters of God.

The third level of need are the things we know inside are sacred and pure, the things we know we need but we can so often lose sight of, or get distracted or scared away from. This need is for the deep things, like love. The need for the real, tangible presence of the true God to manifest in our lives. The need for our purpose on this planet to be revealed. The need to be valued for who we are. The need to make a difference, to be used by God. The needs at this level are in the hearts of everyone (whether acknowledged and known or not) and they don't necessarily require danger or circumstances to get us there. One of the most powerful ways of doing something about this third level of need is by having a posture of the heart that is both *hungry and desperate* for God.

Those who are hungry and desperate will pursue and pursue until they find. They will keep knocking at the door (Luke 11:9).

When you are hungry and desperate for the real thing, you won't accept a knock-off or counterfeit version. When you are looking for something pure and whole, you will make the sacrifices necessary to find what your heart is longing for. In Matthew 13:45-46 we see the parable of the pearl of great value and the merchant who sold everything he had to purchase this one thing. The pearl is the kingdom. It's the Father's house. It's our walk with Him for the rest of time. I have come to see that the most matured and whole sons and daughters of God, the freest, most vibrantly loving people I've ever met, see God and His kingdom this way. It's a precious pearl; nothing else compares to it.

Trials and emergencies will cause us to call upon God; they certainly stir up a desperation and need for Him. Having said that, I believe to be a person who hungers for and desperately needs God, both in trials and also the everyday experiences, is to live at an entirely different level of relationship with Him. This level comes through maturing, and maturing takes a lot of time and a lot of trust moments. We can't escape the maturing process. One healing workshop alone will not do it. A weekend conference by itself will be good, but not enough. A great book might help, but it will only be a piece of the jigsaw. God can do it, if He chooses, in an instant. He could mature us completely with no need for further work, but that is not the way He predominately acts in the Bible, or in our times. He does His work through relationship. That is why we get matured and healed enough to go up to the tenth floor of the building, even though He knows one day we will have to ascend higher. *He wants the relationship so that when that moment comes, we draw on Him and not on ourselves.*

Desperate longing and hunger for God brings us into greater maturity, and one of the fruits of maturity is an increase of desperation and hunger for God.

What is your level of need right now? These last few years of your life, what story do they tell? What would someone say if they stood back and looked at your choices and your decisions?

Are you in a season of planting, of harvesting, or has it been a cold winter that you've just been trying to ride out?

Having emergency emotional or circumstantial needs isn't a lesser category than being hungry and desperate. Every biblical prophet and leader worth preaching about at a church service found themselves in a trial or under pressure at some point and needed to cry out to God. Being in that place is OK – God will use it and do amazing redemptive things through it. But being hungry and desperate for God, willing to go anywhere, do anything, drop anything to do what He asks of you, all to get that precious prize... that is where the greatest healing and freedom is found. That is where the true heart of a child of God is found.

Your heart will be connected to all three levels of need; it will feel the weight of each one of them. That's OK. God wants your heart, so wherever you are on the spectrum of need, you are in the right place to be able to give it to Him today. You might want to spend some time thinking about where you are right now, and where you'd like to be.

The hope is in the finding

For good reasons, many Christians love quoting Jeremiah 29:11:

> For I know the plans I have for you, declares the
> LORD, plans for welfare and not for evil, to give you
> a future and a hope.

God has good plans for us. Plans for prosperity, favour, a hope for our as yet uncertain futures. It is a beautiful verse and a promise I will take for me and my family 100 per cent.

The thing is, though, I have always been more drawn to the couple of verses that follow. As I look at them, I can't help but notice that I never see these on memes or encouraging social media posts. I worry that so much of the Western Church apparently omits or seems oblivious to the fact that these verses are even there:

> Then you will call upon me and come and pray to me, and I will hear you. You will seek me and find me, when you seek me with all your heart. I will be found by you, declares the LORD.
> (vv12-14)

I'm not comparing Bible verses here, but these verse are incredible, maybe even more so than the one that precedes it. My hope for the future comes from the fact that He has said *when I seek Him, I'll find Him.* When all my heart is turned to search and look, to find and discover, to wake early and watch by night for Him, I will find Him. You and I have been told, by God that when we look for Him we're going to find Him. That is a game-changer. God is the prize. Our welfare, our future, our protection from evil is all found by seeking Him and remaining in Him. That is the prize of sonship and daughterhood.

I used to teach the pursuit of destiny and how to follow your calling. I had whiteboards and graphs and flowcharts, you name it. It was all about an approach of progression, out of whatever place we might be in and into a progressive quasi-kingdom lifestyle where you just kept getting closer to the thing you liked doing the most. There was some good in it and my heart was in the right place, but all I taught boiled down to achieving your plans, getting out of the rat race and into your ministry or life sweet spot. I think I had lost sight of what the real prize of being a son was. Yes, God has wonderful plans for us, and yes, He wants us to dream and know our part in His great plan. But being in the presence of our Father, seeking Him and finding Him, and then being *in all of it* with Him – this truly is our great prize.

Waiting for Dad

I was maybe seven years old. My dad had been listening to my brother and me harass him about the latest Lego set that was out. My brother wanted the pirates' galleon. I wanted the governor's mansion. They were a lot of money and I don't quite understand now how it happened, but one week it was revealed that my dad was indeed going to buy these gifts for me and my brother. We were so excited; this was so unheard of. These Lego sets were Christmas-present-level quality – you didn't just get something like this outside a holiday or birthday.

Each evening, around 7pm, I would run up to my room and sit on the windowsill squinting down the road to where my dad would soon turn the corner. For days in a row I would sit there at his homecoming time, waiting for him to turn the corner, praying that he would have a large carrier bag in his hands with my Lego prize in it.

I don't know how many days this went on for, but one beautiful summer's evening, the like of which only exists in your childhood memories, my dad turned the corner onto our road with a huge carrier bag in each hand, the Lego logo clearly visible even from a distance.

I can't describe how much we loved building those Lego sets that night! Dinner time went out the window, probably bedtime too. We had to build them, my brother and me, with our dad's help. For some reason it was really important to be the first to complete the build. Dad went to and from my brother's room and mine, helping us with the tricky parts until late, and the sets were done. Building my Lego governor's mansion with my dad on a warm summer's evening was as good as it sounds.

Here's the thing, though. The next day, after it was all built and complete, at 7pm I ran up to my room and sat on the windowsill and waited for my dad to turn the corner. I did it the next day too, and then the next. I did it for as many evenings as I could remember. For the longest time I kept hoping and praying that he'd turn the corner and have another huge present under his arm for us. After a while, it became clear he wasn't just going to appear with big gifts under his arms after a working day. I was still waiting and watching, though. I kept on doing it and slowly I realised I was just waiting for my dad to come home.

He would come in, say 'hi' to my mum and make his way up the stairs and start changing out of his work clothes and getting ready for dinner. I would sit on the end of his bed and tell him about school and we'd chat about his day. I didn't even know what I was going to talk about; I just knew that I wanted to be around my dad.

He didn't close the door for some 'introvert time'. He didn't go to the study to get on with more important things. He didn't give me an allotted time slot. He didn't ask to see my homework completed before we spoke. He let me find him and be around him.

Long into my late teenage years, when I was in the house at home-coming time, I would still find myself glancing out the window to see if he was coming round the corner; no longer looking for a present under his arm, just looking for him.

I know not everyone's experience of their earthly father was like this, but I share this story to make this point – the joy of sonship is not in the fulfilling of every prophetic word given, nor in making every dream you have come true, though the Father does love it when His children dream big. The joy of living as a son or daughter is that we get Him. Even though the gifts are good, the relationship and the intimacy is better. We may come to Him initially with need, but we stay for the comfort of His presence and the awe of His majesty.

Every chapter of this book has started with an allegorical story of what a relationship with the committed Father could look like. The healing and the dreams and the freedom that come through our journey with Him are so important, as is our sanctification and maturing. He cares about those things deeply. However, more than anything He desires to be sought by us, found by us and connected to us. He desires to be in relationship with us. If He did not want that, then all of our Bibles would have concluded two chapters into Genesis. When humanity fell, God would have just said, 'Well, so much for that idea, I'm off back to heaven, you lot work it out on your own.' This is not what happened. The whole body of Scripture is devoted to God, the 'good shepherd',[104] leading His people back to Himself. That's what the entire book is about. It's all the rescue plan, it's all the bridegroom wooing the bride back, it's all the Father coming back for His kids. To be a son or daughter is to very simply make the choice to remember this truth, to treasure it and anchor our hearts to it. God didn't become Father in the New Testament – it's who He has always been since before time began.

And after it all, I will dwell

Psalm 23 is one of those pieces of Scripture that it seems the world at large knows and finds a quiet hope in. I have seen 'not-yet believers' and members of other religions respond with hope to the words of this psalm. I have seen it used in movies and on TV. Maybe it is the beautiful composition that gets past people's defences. Maybe it is the rawness of its recognition of just how hard things can get and yet that there is hope.

I have read this psalm so many times. I have circled the 'green pastures' and the 'still waters' many times in many different Bibles over the years. I've asked for the restoration of my soul more than a few times. I have walked through that valley and clung to those words, and I have told myself to not fear the evil that was so clearly in my mind. I have sought the protection of God and the guidance of God and I have experienced dining at an abundant table, while all hell is breaking loose outside. I have felt the anointing when I felt barely worthy of it. My cup has overflowed. And the 'goodness

---

[104] John 10:11.

and mercy' of God have remained to this day in hot pursuit of me.

Up to this point I have trailed off and forgotten to even consider the last part of the final verse of the psalm, and what it means for us all. I can't quite believe how many times I've read this psalm and failed to notice the end part of verse 6:

and I shall dwell in the house of the LORD for ever.

The whole psalm is a journey. It's a walk.

One of the most powerful pieces of Scripture for believers throughout the ages, and it is all about a journey.

I am being led.

Along hills and paths that have enough grassy clumps to sustain the walk.

My needs are being thought of.

I'm told to rest.

My restoration is on His mind.

He leads me down paths that He has walked ahead of me.

I get the covering and the glory that He paid for in advance.

The Shepherd leads me through a valley that would intimidate and oppress me were it not for the fact that I am walking by His side.

His strength protects me.

Reassures me.

Guides me.

His abundance doesn't decrease when pressures increase.

He does not cower when enemies mark me as a target.

He anoints me with the oil of olives, grown in a garden and crushed for their essence.

He too stood, crushed, in an olive garden on my behalf.

His mercy overflows.

As I walk, His goodness, His kindness and beauty and forgiveness and mercy follow me hard.

Like sheepdogs that work with a shepherd, they keep me focused on the direction I should be going.

Because at the end of that road there is a house.

Verse 6 says that we will *'dwell* in the house of the LORD' (emphasis mine). A better translation of the first part of this phrase could be 'and I shall return to dwell'.[105] I come back to a place that was always my home. And that place is called 'the house of the Lord'.

After all this time spent in Luke 15, it seems the call to come back home was issued long before Jesus was born in human form and told His parable of a father bringing his two sons home to his house.

This is the house our hearts yearn to dwell in. When we pray for our churches and our towns and cities, it's the home we want them to experience. The feeling of dwelling in this house is what we want people to experience when they step across the threshold into our homes. This home is what we want to see when we close our eyes and pray in the Spirit.

This house is a place of grace; it is where all of you is known and you are loved fiercely. It is a place of truth, where the answers no one else has can be found. It is a place of hope, where despair and defeat are not admitted. It is a place where you can rest. It is a home you can feel secure in. It is a launching pad and a safe harbour. It is somewhere you are going to live in, as well as somewhere you are going to take with you wherever you go, because you carry God inside you. And He carries you inside Him.

> For all who are led by the Spirit of God are sons of God.
> (Romans 8:14)

That's us.

So lean into Him. Let Him love you and love Him back.
Honour Him. Surrender to Him and obey Him.
Welcome Him. Trust Him and live for Him.

---

[105] See ESV footnotes, biblegateway.com (accessed 8th April 2021).

Keep walking with Him and give Him your heart.
Just the heart.
That's all it takes.
It's all He really wants.
You're closer than you think.